JOHN EVELYN AND MRS. GODOLPHIN

MARGARET BLAGGE
From the portrait after Mary Beale at Stonor Park

JOHN EVELYN
AND
MRS. GODOLPHIN

BY

W. G. HISCOCK

LONDON
MACMILLAN & CO. LTD
1951

This book is copyright in all countries which
are signatories to the Berne Convention

PRINTED IN GREAT BRITAIN

To
JO AND MARY

ACKNOWLEDGMENTS

First, to Mr. John Evelyn I am most grateful for his kind permission to publish the letters and other material relevant to the Evelyn – Blagge – Godolphin relationship. To Mr. E. S. de Beer I am indebted for the loan of the proofs of his forthcoming edition of Evelyn's *Diary*, and for his scholarly help and innumerable kindnesses ; I thank the Delegates of the Clarendon Press for allowing me to quote from these proofs. To Mr. A. L. Rowse I am grateful for reading my typescript, making suggestions, and improving it at many points. The Hon. Sherman Stonor very kindly facilitated the inspection and photography of a portrait at Stonor Park. I thank the Governing Body of Christ Church for allowing me to reproduce Smith's engraving of Kneller's portrait of Godolphin, and I thank Mr. G. Cumberlege for permission to quote from the 1939 edition of *The Life of Mrs. Godolphin* (O.U.P.), and to reproduce the Altar of Friendship, an illustration from that edition. Sir Tresham Lever kindly sent me transcripts of three Godolphin letters from the Coventry Papers at Longleat ; I also profited by his knowledge of the Godolphin circle. Finally, I am exceedingly grateful to Mr. J. I. M. Stewart for his kindness and fruitful vigilance in reading my proofs.

CONTENTS

LIST OF ILLUSTRATIONS

NOTE

Original spelling in the quotations has been
adhered to ; punctuation has been added
where necessary.

CHAPTER I

EARLY YEARS

1620–66

THIS study of John Evelyn's friendship covers the years 1669–78, and makes no attempt to add anything of importance to what is already known of the events in his life leading up to it. Therefore only a brief biographical outline of his early years — sufficient to give the reader hitherto unacquainted with Evelyn some knowledge of the man — is attempted.

He was born in 1620 at Wotton, Surrey, in an Elizabethan house set among the hay and corn fields and wooded estates derived from the fortune of his grandfather, who introduced the manufacture of gunpowder into England in the sixteenth century. Fortunately, the country around his home was then, as now, unspoiled ; the nearest powder factories being at Godstone and Long Ditton. At a tender age John roamed the woods, or listened to the village school-master in the porch of Wotton Church — an education belying the family wealth. At ten years of age, he went on to Mr. Snatt's Free School at Southover, near Lewes, where, under the eye of an indulgent grandmother, he stayed too long and learnt too little. After two years with Snatt, John's father wanted him to go to Eton, but, like any other quiet, retiring boy, he was fearful of that school's severe discipline. So he remained with his grandmother and Snatt, regretting it afterwards, and for the rest of his life. As a fellow commoner at Balliol in 1637 his poor schooling prevented his making the best use of what Oxford had to offer. He presented a few books to his college library, and attended the dancing and vaulting classes of the famous (in a way) Mr. Stokes. But even from Mr. Stokes he says he was ' frequently diverted by inclination to newer trifles '. As usual with men of his class, he left Oxford without taking a degree. He wrote the play *Thersander* there (or soon after leaving) and made friends. One of these, James Thicknesse, writing from Oxford in 1640, congratulated him on his ' thrice ingenious play ' and wished that ' applauses may distinguish the scenes of every act '. (However, it has not yet been printed.) In the same year Evelyn became a resident in the Middle Temple, and found his University education ' of very small benefit ' — a remark which does not surprise us. We must realize, however, that Evelyn was prone to magnify trifles, either for or against himself. Evidently he passed through the not uncommon youthful period of moral instability ; he says it was only by the infinite goodness and mercy of God that he did not make shipwreck of his liberty and virtue.

When, on his father's death in 1640, the Wotton estate passed to his elder brother George, Evelyn decided to travel ; having missed both a public school education and the advantages of Oxford, perhaps he hoped to make amends on the continent. Two weeks before embarking for Holland he sat for his portrait to the Dutch painter Henrico van den Borcht who was then living in the Earl of Arundel's household. This likeness turned out to be most attractive, dressed as he was, in elegant clothes of silk, to show his fine, growing taste, his face healthy and virile with no sign of the trials of 1640. Evelyn must have been grateful to the artist, for he got in touch with him at Antwerp a few years later, buying from him prints and pictures, and receiving professional encouragement in his own dilletante efforts at sketching.

Four months in Holland gave him his first taste of sight-seeing but the political portents in England cut it short, forcing him to return in the autumn of 1641. For the first two months of the new year he was in London, ' studying a little, but dancing and fooling more '.

In November he became slightly engaged in the Civil War just after the battle of Brentford ; as his part suggests conscientious objection it will be politic to quote his own words : ' I came in with my horse and arms just at the retreat, but was not permitted to stay longer than the 15th November by reason of the Army's marching to Gloucester, which would have left both me and my brothers expos'd to ruin without any advantage to his Majesty.' On the 10th December he says he ' returned to Wotton, nobody knowing of my having been in his Majesties Army '. In July 1643 he records that he sent a horse, complete with harness, as a gift to the King at Oxford. Evelyn avoided signing the Covenant, and ' finding it impossible to evade the doing very unhandsome things . . . obtained a licence of his Majesty, dated at Oxford and signed by the King, to travel again '. It is remarkable that ' no one ever sought to penalise his curious tepidity '.[1]

Leaving the distasteful military service and his

<hr />

[1] Kate O'Brien, *English Diaries and Journals* (' Impressions of English Literature '), p. 192.

troubled country behind him, he began his education
in earnest. For three years he visited everything worth
seeing, including Paris, Rome, Naples, Venice, Padua,
Verona, Milan, and Geneva, arriving back in Paris in
the autumn of 1646. Thus were laid the foundations
of his knowledge of pictures, engravings, and architecture. He was also mindful of the ancient military glories
of Italy. His friend Thicknesse (who travelled with
him for a while) wrote from England : ' I know each
day you call to mind the ages past and their heroic
actions, and never put foot to ground but in the foot-
steps of a Caesar '.[1] Books were bought and prints
collected. At Padua he matriculated, with excellent
intentions, to study physic and anatomy ; after a few
weeks' work he moved on. But he had one brilliant
idea in Padua in 1645. Obtaining permission of the
anatomist Dr. Vestlingius, the Prefect and Botanic
professor, Evelyn collected from the garden of simples
there, flowers and plants to press into an attractive, fat
folio, each specimen named, and many of them today
still showing the colour that attracted him under the
Italian skies. When Pepys saw it, he said it was ' better
than an herball '.

Evelyn made sketches, in his amateurish way, of
delectable landscapes, and van den Borcht, writing from
Antwerp in 1645 to him at Padua, said : ' If you can
send me any little drafts of your own of the habits of
gentlemen of several places, Mr. Hollar will make them
in print, and make mention that you are the designer
of them '. Two years later the Dutchman dedicated
one of his engravings (after van Dyck) to Evelyn. In
his young manhood Evelyn's health was not at all

[1] Letter, 16th November 1644.

robust, perhaps he was a valetudinarian ; he tells us he
took care to go to bed after being caught in a shower of
rain when nearing Rome — but he had ridden seventy
miles that day. Care was obviously necessary ; Thicknesse says : ' I always judged you of a crystal constitution which the careful owner may preserve as long as
brass, and Venice glasses kept from frost have been
hereditary and as durable as any moveable whatsoever '.[1] So we may say that Evelyn's health was
clear, but brittle as Venice glass, needing care to
preserve it.

But travel palled at times upon his volatile nature ;
at Naples he yearned (and echoed *The Rapture* of
Carew) for homely, marital comforts.

> Happie that man who lives content
> With his own Home and Continent . . .
> But charm'd in down, sleeps by the side
> Of his chast Love, or Loyall Bride
> In whose smooth Arms no sooner hurl'd,
> But he enjoys another world. . . .[2]

On returning to Paris in 1646 Evelyn renewed his
friendship with Sir Richard Browne, the King's resident
ambassador, and Mary his daughter, having first met
them at the outset of his travels. Perhaps he fell in love
with her in 1643, when she was but a child of eight. He
says : ' the prettyness and innocence of her youth . . .
had something methought, in her that pleased me in a
gravity I had not observed in so tender a bud : for I
could call her woman for nothing, but her early steadi-
ness, and that at the age of playing with Babies, she
would be at her Book, her needle, drawing of Pictures,

---

[1] Letter, 27th May 1646.
[2] J. Evelyn, *The State of France*, 1652 : Pref atory Letter.

casting Accompts and understood to govern the house
. . . she began to discourse not impertinently, was
Gay enough for my humour, and one I believed that
might one day grow-up to be the agreable Companion
of an honest-man : But I sweare . . . I had no more
designe to make her my wife, than I had to dive for
pearls upon Salisbury-plaine . . . and yet I made this
Creature my Wife, & found a pearle.' [1] . . . They
were married in 1647 when she was twelve and he was
twenty-seven. Their marriage-day was Corpus Christi,
when the streets of Paris were hung with tapestry and
gay with flowers, strewn as it were in their honour.
About eighteen months later they lived together, first
in Paris and then at Sayes Court,[2] Sir Richard's house
at Deptford.

A few months after the marriage (and before his
wife joined him) Evelyn sent her a curious manuscript,
composed by himself, entitled *Instructions Œconomique*, being thirteen chapters on the ethics of marriage.
It treated of such things as conjugal society, conjugal
offices, the amplification of a family, and included
Francis de Sales's discourse (in French) touching the
nuptial bed. Doubtless Evelyn considered that his
young, inexperienced wife stood in need of such
enlightenment. When he sent it, beautifully bound in
red leather and bearing his arms and motto, *Omnia
explorate, meliora retinete* (prove all things, retain the
best), with his ' most real, unfeigned and inviolable '
love, he gave her implicit instructions to keep it under
lock and key, and to let no other eye peruse it, adding :
' for as none but he which had a mind to blemish his

[1] *The Legend of the Pearle.*
[2] Formerly held on lease from the Crown by Browne ; sequestered
during the Civil War ; purchased by Evelyn in February 1653 for £3,500.

JOHN EVELYN
From the portrait by Robert Walker at Christ Church

honour, would shew his wife naked '. The letter [1] now quoted, which accompanied the manuscript, was also to be kept ' unshown '. Whether we regard this gift as the manifestion of preciosity, a worthy token of practical idealism, or of anything else, the act was typical of Evelyn. The fanciful, manneristic portrait of him by Robert Walker with its frank inscription in Greek : ' repentance is the beginning of wisdom ', and ' those curious hands which enliven Antiquity as well in a Friend, as in a Ruin ' resting upon a death's head (emphasizing the seventeenth-century preoccupation with the idea of Death) accompanied the manuscript.

There was yet another portrait of him, an engraving made in 1650 by the famous French artist Nanteuil.

It seems that Evelyn's children brought him no great happiness : four died early, a most promising son lived only six years, his favourite daughter, Mary, of a ' weak and unsteady disposition ' died at the age of twenty : she who was compact of obedience could yet call her father ' a parent that judges so exactly '. Her fasting brought sickness, and had to be abandoned. ' When my temptations attack me ', she wrote,[2] ' be sure I run immediately to my book with black strings, not delaying and there consult the remedies.' And again : ' When I am dancing, come up & read between four dances and pray.' Another daughter disappointed her parents by making an unfortunate marriage. So ' exactly ' did Evelyn judge her, he refused to visit her as she lay dying. The only surviving son, John, inherited his father's literary talent, was generally in debt, and lacked gust and physical endowment : at nine years of age he had specially fitted boots, armature, and

---

[1] 16th September 1648.   [2] *Rules for spending my pretious tyme well.*

bodice to rectify his poor crooked legs.[1] Lord Berkeley
proved right in saying ' he would never make a leg ' ;
his indifferent health persisted and he died in 1699, seven
years before his father.   Evelyn's wife first conceived
in 1651 at the age of sixteen, and her ninth and last child
was born in 1669, when she was thirty-four and Evelyn
forty-nine.

Sayes Court, a modest triple-gabled Elizabethan
manor house of three storeys, was too near the Deptford
dockyard to develop into an outstandingly attractive
place.   The great dock, twice as long as the house, lay
less than 150 yards away.   On the other side, however,
there were many acres waiting for Evelyn to cultivate,
and grasslands crying out for lime avenues and elm
groves.   Here his schemes were more successful ; here,
in 1653, he also surrounded himself by 250 flourishing
cherry, pear, and apple trees, planted at the ' new
moon, wind W '.   Here (apart from the dockyard) the
ideal could be realized.   Bare acres were transformed
under his skill and direction into a minor show-place.

His skill in landscape gardening may still be seen at
Albury, Surrey, in the terraces planned by him for the
Duke of Norfolk.   Whatever we may think of his
attitude towards military service during the Civil War,
he did not lack physical courage : on Christmas Day,
1657, in Exeter House Chapel, he persisted in receiving
the Holy Communion with the muskets of Commonwealth troops pressed against his body.   And if at home
he lived the life of a country gentleman he also loved
his study.

Horace Walpole's succinct testimony of Evelyn's

[1] Agreement, 21st March 1661, for £130 between Hermen Schot and
Evelyn for the cure and apparatus.

writings can hardly be bettered : ' The works of the
Creator and the mimic labours of the creature were all
objects of his pursuit. He unfolded the perfection of
the one and assisted the imperfections of the other.'

In his *Sculptura*, published in 1662, his wide knowledge of, and enthusiasm for engraving — an enthusiasm
born on his travels abroad — must have inspired many
to begin print-collecting. Men like Henry Aldrich,
Dean of Christ Church, took advantage of the book —
the first in English on the subject — and left to his
college a collection second only in interest and extent
to the later collection at Chatsworth. *Sculptura* is a
dull and difficult book, little more than a compilation
of artists' names and subject-matter ; nevertheless we
must acknowledge its great share in forming two other
private collections, those of Ashmole and Pepys, though
we cannot believe that Pepys ever waded through the
Sculptura. However, Evelyn wrote to him about
collecting, advising him to collect engraved portraits
and miscellaneous prints.

Of Evelyn's other works published during his early
years, *Sylva* (1664) gave him his high contemporary
reputation (for it must be remembered that the *Diary*
remained in manuscript until the early nineteenth
century). *Sylva* was a piece of propaganda for the
reafforestation of Great Britain, and his most successful
book. In his mock-modest fashion, he says it is the
work of ' a plain husbandman and a simple forester '.
But it had a tremendous effect. In his own words he
' incited a world of planters to repair their broken
estates ' — estates impoverished largely by the Civil
War. Woods and avenues sprang up everywhere.
Although the greater part of the timber woods have

been cut down, the hearts of oak carried the British flag all over the world. We might almost say that the Battle of Trafalgar was won in Evelyn's study at Deptford.

Obviously he possessed a genius for looking ahead of the immediate wants of his generation. He was the first man to record the greatness of Wren. He discovered the skilful wood-carver Grinling Gibbons, encouraged him, and found him patrons. What a proud moment it was for Evelyn in February 1671, when he took his friends Pepys and Wren, after entertaining them to dinner at Sayes Court, to see the wonderful craftsman's copy of Tintoretto's Crucifixion. It is a conjecture that President Bathurst, of Trinity College, Oxford, and a friend of Evelyn, employed Gibbons for the exquisite reredos in the college chapel at Evelyn's suggestion. As a token of his gratitude, Gibbons presented Evelyn with a table decorated with characteristic carvings of fruit, flowers, and foliage.

He published another important work in 1664, the *Parallel between Ancient and Modern Architecture*, a translation from the French of Fréart de Chambray (and probably the best work on Renaissance architecture written in the seventeenth century), to which Evelyn added *An Account of Architects and Architecture*. Now Evelyn's *Account* is comparatively well known, and freely quoted to show his dislike of Gothic. He said ' all the mischiefs and absurdities in the modern structures proceed chiefly from our busie and Gothick triflings in the composition of the Five Orders '. This phrase, and particularly the word ' busy ' is always associated with Evelyn and Gothic. It stuck in the architectural conscience. Wren remembered it seventeen years later ; when planning

Tom Tower to agree with Wolsey's Gothic, he said :
' I have not continued so busy as he began '. In a later
edition of the *Parallel*, which Evelyn dedicated in 1697
to Wren, he expanded his criticisms of Gothic, and gave
us two more memorable phrases : he spoke of ' heavy,
dark, melancholy, and monkish piles ' with their ' lace
and other cut-work, and crinkle crankle '.

Evelyn was enthusiastic for the new classicism, Inigo
Jones's Banqueting House (now the Royal United
Service Institution) and Wren's Sheldonian, St. Paul's,
and Trinity College, Cambridge, and pleaded for the
general resuscitation of classical architecture. Blomfield
has said that ' Evelyn's judgment was sound and there
can be little doubt that in publishing this treatise he did
a great service to the architecture of his time. He called
attention to the fact that there is such a thing as grammar
in architecture . . . and he helped to restore architecture to its rightful place as a learned art.' That is quite
true. And it should be noted that Wren's first full
Renaissance buildings, Pembroke College, Cambridge,
and the Sheldonian, and Evelyn's *Account* appeared or
were designed in 1664. Evelyn should also be credited
with diagnosing the *malaise* of the unlearned masons
who had been brought up in the mediaeval tradition ;
that they were suffering from architectural indigestion
as a result of faulty assimilation of such works as Serlio
and Sir Henry Wotton's uncritical *Elements of Architecture*
(1624). Evelyn saw that the days of the master masons
were numbered, and there is an interesting echo of his
discontent — again in the Tom Tower correspondence
— when Wren refers to ' some Oxford artists [masons,
obviously] of whose powers he could not boast '.
When Evelyn restated in the *Account* the qualities of an

architect as laid down in Vitruvius he made, in effect, the first call for the ' individual ' architect. The buildings and the scholarship of Inigo Jones and Wren had shown that there was no going back to the unlettered mason, and Evelyn makes clear his view of this development. He pleaded also that ' our gentry ' be conversant with the art, a plea not unconnected, perhaps, with the advent of the amateur architect towards the end of the seventeenth century.

There is one curious aberration in Evelyn's plea for the classical architecture. He does not distinguish between the pure Palladianism of Inigo Jones and the early work of Wren. He brackets the Banqueting House with the Sheldonian. Perhaps this apparent blindness was general, and to be explained by the immense prestige of Wren as the arrived and individual architect, the scholarly, professional architect, and that Evelyn as a close friend of Wren preferred not to point out the purer classicism of the Banqueting House. Again it may have been Evelyn's adulation of Wren or the prestige of Wren which delayed the revival of the strict Palladianism. However that may be, Christ Church, the college which now most appropriately finds a home for Evelyn's library, gave a perfect monument to his precepts when Dean Aldrich designed Peckwater Quadrangle in 1705. And thus — when Wren was nearing the end of his career — was bridged the gap between Inigo Jones and the Palladianist revival.

Soon after these last two publications were off his hands, Evelyn had to attend to more serious and dangerous business. In the autumn and winter of 1665 when thousands of Londoners were dying of the Plague every week, he sent his wife and family to Wotton,

and stayed at his post as a Commissioner to continue
his care of the sick and wounded prisoners arising out
of the Dutch War. Then, a year later, he writes of the
Fire of London, and displeases us ; it is done ' so
admirably, so vividly, with a detachment that is just
a shade too cold, too touched with carefulness '.[1]

[1] Kate O'Brien, *English Diaries and Journals* ('Impressions of English
Literature'), p. 193.

CHAPTER II

MAIDS OF HONOUR

1669–72

In 1669 Evelyn first sought the friendship of the Maids of Honour at Court, an interest which apparently coincided with the end of the business of raising a family.

He says he was perfectly contented with his wife ; indeed she made ' the best wife in the world, sweet, and (though not charming) agreeable, and as she grew up, pious, loyal, and of so just a temper, obliging and withall discreet, as has made me very happy '.[1]

Perhaps in his wife's lack of charm we shall find the reason for his quest of friendship. Or, like Francis Finch, he may have felt that ' while one can adore a mistress, affect her for a wife, yet believe her not so proper for all the relations of Friendship ', for ' unless the love proceed to a friendship, it is short of what it might have come to '.[2] He was perfectly open with her ; this matter of friendship was a subject of conversation between them, and she freely gave him ' the liberty to converse with other ladys and to make virtuous friendships with the sex '.[1] At one time she actually encouraged it, as we shall see later. We notice, however, that the endings of his letters to her by this time made a decrescendo from ' unfeigned, inviolable love ' to ' yours J. E.' or to being unsigned.

Evelyn was both learned and extraordinarily devout.

---

[1] *The Legend of the Pearle.*   [2] *Friendship*, 1654.

He was also an artist in spirit (if not in practice) and a virtuoso. But in 1669 he was aware of his physical shortcomings : ' I was a man of the shade,' he says, ' and one who had convers'd more amongst plants and Books, than in the Circles : I had contracted a certain odd reservedness, which render'd me wholly unfit to converse among the knights of the Carpet, and ye refinéd things of the Antechambers : some said I was morose, and affected, others that I was plainly stupid and a fop '.[1] Evidently he lacked some of his former youthful spirit or an aptitude for the life of the Court.

But we cannot quite believe his depreciatory remarks, for he spent the greater part of each week in the vicinity of Whitehall. There were council meetings of the Foreign Plantations or of the Royal Society, Lord Arlington or the Archbishop of Canterbury to dine with, sermons to hear, Treasury payments to be sought on some outstanding bill for the care of the sick and wounded prisoners, a copy of one of his publications to be presented to the King or to have a chat with him on an antiquarian topic ; in fact, in the Court season or when on a visit to the coast to see one of his Deputy Commissioners, he spent little more than the week-ends at his ' poor, quiet villa ' at Sayes Court.

We imagine him careful rather than elegant in his dress, of middle stature, with fine eyes set in a face not to be judged handsome on account of a nose a trifle too long.

In the antechambers of Whitehall the Maids of Honour were in no haste to engage him in conversation ; they said he had ' a forbidding countenance '[2]

---

[1] *The Legend of the Pearle.* [2] *Op. cit.*

and were rather afraid of him ; indeed, some took him for a schoolmaster. He went so far as to believe they thought his wife the unhappiest woman in the world — but that is typical hyperbole. She was certainly some-what remote from him, busy with her family, and the cares of baking, preserving, and stilling, finding her chief recreation in writing excellent letters regularly and over a long period to her son's tutor, Dr. Ralph Bohun of New College. She was also diverted by her ardent admirers, Sir Samuel Tuke (a cousin) and her brother-in-law William Glanvill — a widower for some years.

On a June day of 1669, Mrs. William Howard, daughter-in-law of the Earl of Berkshire, accompanied Mrs. Evelyn on a pleasure trip down the Thames estuary, the party including Mrs. Howard's seventeen-years-old daughter Dorothy, and her friend of the same age, Margaret Blagge. On other occasions the two girls visited Sayes Court as playfellows of Evelyn's children, bringing with them Anne Howard, Dorothy's fourteen-years-old sister. Evelyn also saw the young people and Mrs. Howard at Whitehall ; the latter as housekeeper to the Duchess of York, Dorothy and Margaret as Maids of Honour ; and Anne became a Maid of Honour to the Queen in 1673.

Evelyn showed no particular interest in Dorothy, and apart from naming her *Alcidonia* for her calm temperament, prudence, and beauty, tells us little about her. It was Anne, with her wit and vitality, who first attracted him. At Whitehall, she was the cynosure of the gallants, with her 'thousand pretty impertinen-cies'. The critical Evelyn thought her 'not a little affected', but, captivated with the rest, could not but

admire. Not for the same reason as the gallants, though ;
he says ' that which most deeply engag'd my peculiar
esteeme was a piece of solemn devotion she had composed for the regulation of her owne life that I found
by chance upon her table, and which, unheeded by her,
I had perused '. Thus he made sure his friendship was
firmly founded. Here was a Restoration rarity, a
young lady who could be at once merry and religious.
After the fashion of the matchless Orinda, Mrs. Philips,
and her Platonic friends of the 1650's, he named her
Ornithia (the bird-like). This friendship, however, did
not develop ; she remained his ' playfellow ', perhaps
because she was rather young, or maybe the gallants
got more of her time than Evelyn. But she did inspire
one short unfinished piece of writing [1] in which he
renamed her *Penthea* (the sad) and gave himself the
name *Philaretes* (a lover of virtue). And in a few lines
of verse, Evelyn implies that Anne objected to her change
of name. Perhaps she was sad because Evelyn had
transferred his affections — or was about to do so.

TO ORNITHIA

Why deare *Ornithia*, art thou so perverse ?
In Rymes so gentle, and in Prose so fierce ?
Domestic strife, and forraine War to wage
At once, is not hostillity, but Rage ;
Whilst I the faire *Penthea* still adore
Be you *Ornithia* as you were before :
And since two kingdomes now for peace prepare
Let us all acts of Variance forbeare,
And the calm *Alcidonia* mediate : Words
Pierce deeper in a Lover's heart, than Swords.
Go forlorn paper then to th' cruel faire,
Yet go not alltogether in Despaire :

[1] *The Legend of the Pearle.*

Perhaps, when she has heard thee pleade my Cause,
She may reverse my doome, and juster Laws
Impose : But if she for *Penthea's* sake
Condemn this gentle Martyr to the stake,
And still inrag'd, thy wronged Lord despise,
Thou canst not fall a nobler Sacrifice.

From *Otium Evelyni*, p. 58

Here is a letter [1] from Anne Howard to Evelyn in which she hits off a character in a sentence, and in a few lines brings to life the whole family circle of Sayes Court, including her critical elders. No wonder they called her ' ranting Nanny ' :

' Most conestant and Loving playfellow I was I confesse in deepe mortification having banisht all thoughts both past and presant of the vanityes of Sayis court — abesence and the mulligrubes begining now to cure those feates of acttivity I wonce playd thare : but I find mor ose [morosity] is neaver to be forgoten yet as soon as I parceved my self gowing to such maturity and wisdom I thought it might be no small favoer to give you the titell of my frind insted of playfelow and ranting nany : thus was I becom a new cretuer : and full of soberiety when in comes the humbel pietiction [2] [petition] as I thought of John Evellin esqier : which I had no sooner parusd but all thees good resoluetions vanishit and vanety wonce more took posession for which it had a large subject : together with hard wordes : and supeurfin compilements which you know ganes much upon the weaker vessill : esspassally when told wone by a man of conscience : then on the other sid it brought into my memory the begining of my victory over that second dioginus [3] [w]hom with much

[1] 20th November 167-.
[2] Probably an invitation to nurse Evelyn's daughter, Elizabeth.
[3] Perhaps Sir Gabriel Sylvius, whom she married 13th November 1677.

labour I have at last brought in subj[e]ction to my will
and made a very grig : ¹ not forgetting the meny suites
of slim,² the great variete of stokins gloves and crispe ³
with all the rest of that brockery ⁴ waier : as also
Sellingares round ⁵ in sipits which wee have here to
fore so merily traced : so that I am now as full of
mischife as ever, therefor look to your self play-fellow
for I shall com lick [like] a lion broke loos from his
den and play more trickes than robin goodfellow.'

Now she breaks into ' rymes so gentle ' ; yet they
are not so gentle as Evelyn had led us to expect.

> for do not think becaus you say
> that littiel Blagg ⁶ as bright as day
> nor all the rest of the court splendoer
> could make to playfellow your love less tender
> shall keepe you saffe within your tub
> for I will com with a dub a dub dub
> nor shall sr Richard Browen ⁷ that knight
> Ore rather that most sleepe wight
> hoo ere the day has done ites dawen
> first strechis out a grievous yawen
> then calles du Bourg ⁸ bides him com light
> for he'll to bed ' Layedayes good night '
> nor madam Evellines ⁹ jelous eye
> hoo lives so curcomspect and lookes so shy
> nor Jack ¹⁰ in frock that hermit poor
> in want of super so demuer
> nor Bohune ¹¹ that quintisence of sniff and spleen
> my foe so mortall and so keene

---

¹ A merry person. ² Thin, flimsy fabric.
³ Material for veils or head-covering. ⁴ Brokery.
⁵ Sellinger's Round, a piece of music for the maypole. See Preface
to Evelyn's *Mundus Muliebris*, 1690 : ' they danc'd the Canarys, Spanish
Pavan, and Selengers Round upon Sippets '.
⁶ Margaret Blagge. ⁷ Sir Richard Browne, Evelyn's father-in-law.
⁸ Sir R. Browne's servant. ⁹ Mrs. Evelyn.
¹⁰ John Evelyn, jun.
¹¹ Edmund Bohun, of New College : tutor to J. Evelyn, jun.

nor yet dame Turners [1] hoge nor bour
the Porters ferese [2] of brick closse [3] doer
shall have the power to part us twain
whillest in Dedford [4] I remain
for when my time of nursinges over
I'll turn agane an arant rover
then we'll laugh and drink good sheaary
and spend the nights with harts full mery
from my closit so well adoorend [adorned] with
        hood [5] in dollful [doleful]
maner this 20 of november.

We are to believe that none of the 'spoil-sports' of
Deptford, the ageing, yawning Sir Richard Browne, the
jealous Mrs. Evelyn, or her sniffing friend Bohun can
part Anne Howard from Evelyn during her return to
the scene of former frolics. Nor does she believe that
'littiel Blagg' and the rest of the Court could make
Evelyn's love for her less tender. Now can we see why
she objected to the transition from *Ornithia* to *Penthea*.
What an attractive creature she must have been ! Alas,
Sayes Court inspired no more epistolary gems like this ;
in 1677, when she was twenty-one (having learnt
perhaps, from Evelyn, the attractions of middle-age),
she married the forty-five-years-old Sir Gabriel Sylvius,
who, taking her to Holland, dwindled her into an
ordinary letter-writer and a childless, perhaps discontented, wife.

We may say that Evelyn gathered no laurels when,

[1] Mrs. Evelyn's still-house woman (see letter from R. Bohun to Mrs.
Evelyn, 26th October 1675).

[2] Query 'fairies', a satirical term for Mr. Porter's children. He was
a tenant of Evelyn's.

[3] 'Brick Close' was part of the forecourt of Evelyn's residence, Sayes
Court.

[4] Deptford.

[5] The hood, which covered half her face, was evidently considered
unbecoming.

adhering to his motto *Omnia explorate, meliora retinete*
(prove all things, retain the best), he allowed Anne's
friend Margaret Blagge to usurp his affections in 1672 —
but it is quite likely that that happened. She was one of
the four daughters of Colonel Thomas Blagge and Mary,
the daughter of Sir Roger North, both of ancient
Suffolk families. In 1658, when six years old, Margaret
journeyed to Paris with the Duchess of Richmond, who
placed her under the care of the Catholic Countess of
Guildford until the Restoration. As Margaret was
confirmed when eleven years of age by Bishop Gunning,
who was deeply moved by her religious proficiency, we
may assume that she was naturally devotional — and
despite the influence of the Countess of Guildford
devoted to the Church of England. In 1666 she became
a Maid of Honour to the Duchess of York, and on the
latter's death in 1671, transferred her services to Her
Majesty.

Mrs. Evelyn, who had few favourites and whose
motto seems to have been ' no virtue, no favour ',
recognized Margaret's singular character long before
Evelyn was attracted by her ; in fact, continual persuasion and enlightenment by both herself and Anne
Howard proved necessary before he fell for her charms.
At Court, Margaret had the reputation of a saint, and
deserved it. To rise early for prayer she would instruct
a sentry to pull at an appointed hour, a thread passed
through her bedroom keyhole and attached to her arm.
Her daily work, founded on a scheme of devotion, put
God before all else. Her scheme was headed : ' My
life, by God's Grace, without which I can do nothing '.
There were thoughts and prayers to be used whilst
dressing, and such as, ' When I go into the with-

C

drawing room, let me consider what my Calling is :
To entertain the Ladies, not to talk foolishly to men :
more especially the King '. Her naïveté was charming,
and her moral courage great : ' Be sure never to talk to
the King when they speak filthily, tho' I be laughed
at '. She was humble too : ' If you speake anything
they like, say 'tis borrowed : may the Clock, the
Candle, may everything I see, teach and instruct me
some thing '.[1] She had a trick of pinning up a slip of
paper in any corner to remind her of some special care
or obligation.

If in a Court notorious for its lack of morality Anne
Howard was a rarity, Margaret was unique. With
others, the body came first, with Margaret the soul.
Herein lay her attraction for the devout Evelyn, though
after some long continuance of his scepticism as to her
exceptional way of life. But eventually his eulogies
were joined to those of Anne and Mrs. Evelyn, the latter
remarking that ' never were two people more alike in
way and inclination ' : opportunities (brought about
by Anne and Dorothy) of divining Margaret's steadfast
nature as he listened to ' her pretty conversation ',
forced a conclusion that ' she indeed might not be that
pert Lady ' he had fancied. When Evelyn was ready to
express his budding approval, Margaret — favourably
impressed by Evelyn herself — soon afforded opportunities for him to visit her at Whitehall.

She possessed physical attractions, too. Evelyn says
she was young, elegant, charming, a beauty, and witty
enough to reprove his own moroseness : all these, ' and
greatly devout ', he adds, ' which put me out of all feare

---

[1] *The Life of Mrs. Godolphin*, by John Evelyn (ed. by H. Sampson,
1939), pp. 14-17.

of her Raillery, and made me looke upon her with extraordinary respect '.[1] She was possessed of exquisite taste, and her friends ' the greatest Duchesses and Ladies . . . sought her friendship and assistance upon any occasion of solemn pomp, masque or ball. . . . She had all the pretty arts and innocent stratagems imaginable of mingling serious things on all occasions . . . wherever she came she made virtue and holiness a cheerful thing, lovely as herself '.[2]

Was she a beauty ? The two known portraits are dissimilar : Matthew Dixon painted her in 1673, un-flatteringly, in workaday dress, an abigail's hair-style, and with downcast eyes that are silent. Mary Beale (of the Lely School) gave her (perhaps a year later) more distinction, fine silks, artificial curls, and a pleasing, thoughtful, wide-eyed expression. If Mary Beale's portrait is the more faithful, there is considerable justification for Evelyn turning from the boisterous charm of 'ranting Nanny' ; but if not, none, though only, of course, by ordinary standards.

Their friendship, however, was to prove extra-ordinary.

[1] *Life*, p. 21.   [2] *Life*, p. 100.

CHAPTER III

THE ALTAR OF FRIENDSHIP
1672

'NEVER were two people more alike in way and inclination', said Mrs. Evelyn. Evelyn was the master, Margaret the pupil, religion their study. Margaret's readiness to become his protégée is perfectly understandable. Her case was like that of an art student, a novice without technique, but intensely devoted to painting, suddenly finding herself under the guidance of an Old Master who recognized an apt and eager pupil. No wonder she succumbed, and caught the opportunity to strengthen and cement their friendship. In the autumn of 1672 she told Evelyn she 'had never a friend in the world'. This utterance was Evelyn's opportunity. In Margaret he saw the two elements that were missing in his wife : charm and an aptitude for religion.

When Margaret made this confession, they were together in her neatly furnished chamber in Whitehall, where she kept her oratory — probably a silk-covered table bearing a crucifix or painting, that stood like a recessed altar, in the wall-arcading. As in a Rembrandt etching, the fading light of that October afternoon shed a gleam upon the silken cloth, breathing an air of ritual. A new life lay before her. Had she forgotten Sidney Godolphin ? All the Court knew that six years ago they had met, and that their engagement

which followed had stood like a rock. After his election
as member of parliament for Helston in 1668, he was
nearly always abroad as a special envoy in France or
Flanders. Just now — at the age of twenty-seven — he
was following the French Court during the campaign.
He had the nickname of Bacon Face, being of a pink
and excessively fair complexion. So careful, calculating
and unobtrusive was he, always waiting his chance to
be useful, the King said of him : ' He is never in the
way, and he is never out of the way'. He must have
been rather like that in his association with Margaret.
But there is no evidence that his frequent absence
made her fonder. Yet no other claimed her affections,
nor was it likely to happen ; for a Maid of Honour
that kept her love for the absent, would inspire little
in those present at Court — especially when safe-
guarded by such superlative virtue as hers. So, naturally
enough, on this October afternoon, Evelyn asked her :
' What do you esteem a certain gentleman beyond
the seas to be ? ' Margaret, as an engaged woman of
some years' standing, gave — in Evelyn's words — a
curiously inadequate answer : ' Alas . . . he is very
ill and that makes me very much concern'd : But
I don't speak to you of him : whom God will, I
hope, be gracious to : But I would have really a
Friend, and in that name is a great deal more than I can
express : A Faithful Friend, whom I might trust with
all I have, and God knows that's but little : For him
whom you mean, cares not to meddle with my concerns ; nor would I give him the trouble.' [1]

We must understand that in *The Life of Mrs.
Godolphin* Evelyn is writing after Margaret's death and

[1] *Life*, p. 22.

for two specific audiences, Lady Sylvius (formerly our lovable Nan Howard) and Godolphin, and that in this extract Evelyn is justifying his own indispensability as a friend : and there will be other passages which require the same consideration.

'Madame,' replied Evelyn, 'do you say this to me, as if I were capable of serving you in any thing considerable and in my power ? ' To which Margaret said : ' I believe you the person in the world who would make such a friend, had I merit enough to deserve it '. Such confidence opened his heart, and somewhat carried him away to enlarge upon all the definitions of friendship. ' Understand ', he concluded, ' that friend in the way you mean is the nearest relation in nature.' Here she became critical of his wordiness, saying, with a smile : ' Pray leave your definitions, compliments, and distinctions, and be my friend then in earnest ; and look upon me henceforth as your child (if that relation be so near) and call me so '.

The moment of ritual, the rite of friendship had arrived. Taking pen and ink upon the table, Evelyn drew something on a paper, like an altar ; with a heart upon it surrounded by a halo of stars, writing : ' Be this the symbol of inviolable friendship ', and presented it to her, with the pen, which she took, and subscribed : ' Be it so : Margaret Blagge, 16 Octob. 1672 ', and then gave it to him with a smile.

If to Margaret the pact at this moment seemed serious enough, to Evelyn it was sacred. ' Do you know what you have done ? ' he said. ' You have brought yourself into bonds you can never untie whilst you live : the title that has consecrated this altar, is the marriage of Souls . . . friendship is beyond all relations

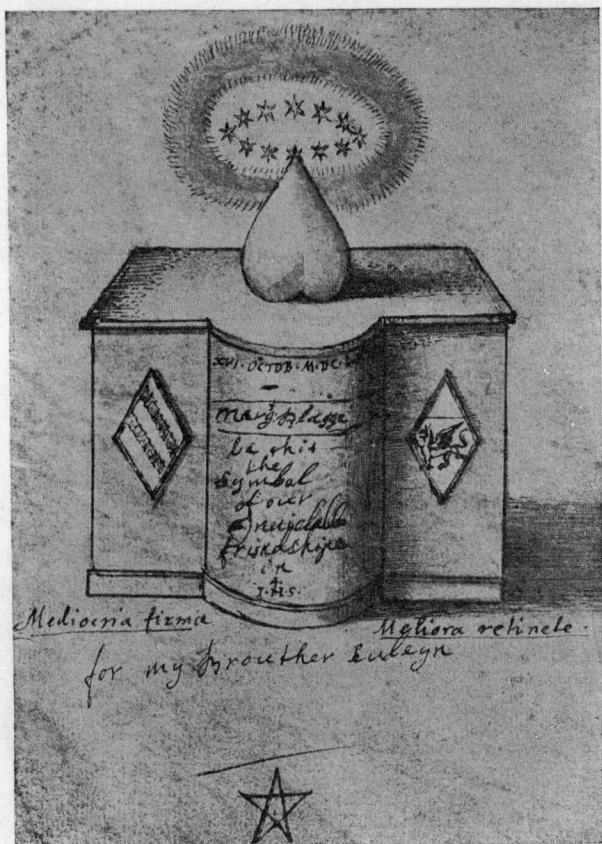

THE ALTAR OF FRIENDSHIP
From a drawing in Evelyn's *Diary*

of flesh and blood, because it is less material : there is
nature, and consanguinity in that of parents and kindred:
but the friendship is of course, and without inherent
virtue : for which reason (and that 'tis accidental) the
conjugal state itself is not altogether the most happy. . . .'
Evelyn continued in a vein that seems one-sided, though
doubtless accidentally so. ' You entitle me ', he said,
' to all that you can with honour and religion part with
in this world.' Margaret, the twenty years' old novitiate
could only ask : ' What am I to do ? ' With something
of Congreve's rhythm, Evelyn, the master, went on :
' The privileges I claim in virtue of that *character* are,
that I may visit you without being thought impor-
tunate, tho' perhaps sometimes impertinent : That I
may, now and then, write to you, to cultivate my style :
discourse with you, to improve my understanding, read
to you, to receive your reflections ; and that you freely
command me upon all occasions, without any reserve
whatsoever : you are to write to me, when absent.
Mention me in all your prayers to God ; to admonish
me of all my failings : to visit me in sickness, to take
care of me when I am in distress, and never to forsake
me ; change or lessen your particular esteem, 'till I
prove unconstant, or perfidious, and no more a friend :
in short there is (as I said) in friendship, something
of all relations and practical duties, and something above
them all : these madam, are the laws, and they are
reciprocal and eternal.' [1]

According to Evelyn, Margaret had little more to
say that day : ' when next you come, I will tell you ',
she said, ' what I have for you to do in good earnest '.
However, if she had had the wit with which he credits

[1] *Life*, p. 24.

her would she not have interrupted his law-giving, and
said : ' cultivate your style ? Why, you are already
a writer ! ' And he might have replied thus : ' I am
but an ingenious drudge, a recorder of facts, in architecture, engraving, planting ; I might have written as well
as Thomas Browne of Norwich if my poor spirit had
been a little raised ; but I have done a deal of gardening,
and gardening interferes with writing.' When he said :
' Admonish me of all failings ', it is to be hoped that
she replied, with some liveliness : ' I know at least of
one failing ; you are a little mock-hypocrite ! For
instance, you speak of *Sayes Court* as your " poor quiet
villa ", which is indeed a lovely place, and you are very
proud of it ! ' With an indulgent smile, he would have
said : ' I believe you are right, my child : yes, I *am*
proud of it ; the acres are few, but sweet '. So, like
the greatest and wisest of Romans, Evelyn dedicated an
altar to Friendship : and went back to his Whitehall
lodgings with a light step, and a quickened sense of
life. As he walked his spirit soared. ' What sweetness
is there in the exercise of natural love ? . . . The delight
which a pair of special faithful friends do find in loving
and engaging one another is a most pleasing, sweet
delight ' : Evelyn marked the passage in Baxter's *The
Saint's Everlasting Rest*.[1] He also commemorated the
pact in verse :

> Would ye now know my Angel's name ?
> All that is choice in Natures frame :
> All that or Grace, or Good commends
> In this deare Saint of mine Transcends :
> By *Friendships* sacred Tie combin'd,
> Devoted, and by *Symbol* sign'd ;

[1] 1669 ed., p. 756.

With Hand and Seale, & solemn Oath,
To *Jesu*, we ourselves betroth :
Witnesse the *Day, Moneth, Yeare, Ring, Vow,*
This *Book*,[1] *Crosse, Altar, Heart,* & Thou
(*Lover of Men*) who dost impart
Such love, and shed it in our Heart :
How often, ah ! deare Lord ! has She
Her pure hands lifted-up to Thee !
With what bright Flames of Heavn'ly fire
Have I beheld her Soule aspire !
Winged with Zeale, & Rap't with Love
Looke up to meete the Heavenly Dove !
Ah ! Book belov'd ! how oft have you
Drenched in Teares of pearly Dew
Shed by this Holy Penitent,
Made my obdurate Heart to rent !
How often to the Altar led
My Saint hast Thou accompanied !
When 'ere Celestial Food we took,
Thou allways wer't her darling Book :
When e're we travell'd by the Way,
She was still wont in Thee to pray.
In Bed, before the Morning light,
Still Thou would'st be her soules delight,
And when soft-Sleepe did close her eyes,
Learn'd *Andrews* in her bosome lies :
O then Deare Dearest Book to me,
Next Sacred Writ, I'll cherish Thee.
Ne're will I sleepe, ne're will I wake
Without Thee for the *donor's* sake :
Kindle but in my Heart that fire
And like her (Lord) my Zeale inspire,
So shall we both with Blessings Crown'd
Thine everlasting Prayse resound.
                    Alleluja !
          Amen.

          From *Otium Evelyni*, p. 127.

[1] L. Andrewes, *Book of Devotions.* The Book and the Cross did not
appear in the original drawing of the Altar of Friendship.

Evelyn says in the *Life* that Margaret wrote to him ' a little after ' giving her thoughts on the compact : she says she understood something of the Office of Friendship before she knew him, and believes she will need little instruction. ' You are then my first friend ', she continues ; ' the first that ever I had, and ever shall be so . . . I believe I shall never lay down my resolution of continuing yours, but with my life : I thankfully accept your counsel and will endeavour to follow it.' We see that she could, occasionally, hit upon a choice or charming phrase : ' But birds themselves have always the good nature to teach their young ones, and so must you '. It seems likely that she knew something of Francis Finch's *Friendship* (1654) : ' Friendship is virtuous ; for indeed nothing that is not so is or can be lasting '. Perhaps she remembered those words when she said to Evelyn : ' I would have nothing that passes between us, to have any resemblance of Friendships which do not last '. She doubts her ability to give advice or to be useful to Evelyn, unless to serve him ' as an act of humility ', concluding, ' till death reckon me your friend '.

As these passages are but portions of two letters, one undated, the other an anniversary letter written in October 1673, it is at once plain that Evelyn's chronology in the *Life* is faulty, and that there were other aspects of the early stages of their friendship passed over by him in that compilation. Indeed, Margaret's undated letters (in the writing of which she rarely took pen from paper) constitute an array of jigsaw pieces, and to fit them into Evelyn's picture of her is a task made excessively difficult by the faulty detail and perspective of the *Life* ; in fact, when assembled, the letters make a very

different picture, as we shall see. Additional high lights
from Evelyn's various pieces of writing composed for
Margaret's use, will be seen to add to the illumination
of *his* character.

When she writes : ' What you mean by making a
figure I can't tell, unless it be that I signify nothing to
you ; I wish I did with my hart but how can I help it ,'
it is apparent that the possessive Evelyn has determined
to ' improve ' her ; that the master has taken the pupil
in hand. So she suggests : ' Put but your method into
blake and whit and I will obey you '. A delicate question was answered : the propriety of his proposed
weekly visits — generally on Tuesday — satisfactorily,
too, as far as Evelyn was concerned ; Margaret assured
him ; ' I will not confine your visits, no though you
shold desier me, and yet truly I seldom trouble anybody
against ther wills. When I lookt contracted, I was
never nearer in my life disolving ; therefore you se
you are not spild in my face, though you are in my soul.'
In other words, her engagement to Godolphin is not
binding, her attachment to Evelyn is spiritual and if he
wants to visit her, he may do so.

In the *Life* [1] Evelyn gives Margaret's account, in his
own words, of how her affection for Godolphin had
changed : ' He [Godolphin] was sent abroad by his
Majesty, and fell sick, which gave me greate trouble —
and I allow'd more time for prayer, & the performance
of holy duties, than ever before I had ever done ; and
I thank God, found infinite Pleasure in it, far beyond all
other ; and I thought lesse of foolish things, that us'd
to take up my time.

' Being thus chang'd myselfe, and liking it so well, I

[1] Pp. 30-31.

earnestly begged God that he would impart the same satisfaction to him I loved : 'tis done (my friend) 'tis done, and from my soule, I am thankfull : And tho' I believe he loves me passionatly yet I am not where I was. My place is fill'd up with Him, who is All in All. I find in him none of that tormenting Passion to which I neede sacrifice myselfe : But still, were we disingag'd from the world, we should marry, under such restraints as were fit ; and by the agreeableness of our humour, make each other happy. But at present, there are obstructions : He must perpetualy be enagag'd in businesse, and follow the Court, and live allways in the world, and so have lesse time for the service of God, which is a sensible affliction to him : wherefore, we are not determined to precipitate that matter ; but to expect a while, and see how things will go ; having a greate mind to be together, which cannot with decency be don, with the marriage ; nor that, to either of our satisfactions, without being free from the world : in short, serving of God is our end : and if we cannot do that quietly together, we will asunder . . . and if we can but passe our younger-yeares, 'tis not likely, we shall be much concern'd for marriage when old. . . . In a word, if we marry, it will be to serve God, and to encourage one another ; if we do not, 'tis for that end too. . . . '

Evelyn goes on to make the important statement that he opposed Margaret's desire for celibacy : ' This [the foregoing], being the consequence of some Discourse, and serious Debate, in which I had oppos'd a Melancholy Resolution she now and then Entertain'd me with, of absolutely Renouncing the thoughts of Marriage. . . .' We shall see presently, what his equivocal opposition amounted to.

Though the twenty-years-old Margaret could be soft and melting at her devotions, she probably showed in sexual matters, not frigidity, but some physical aversion. In consequence, there was little risk of her friendship with Evelyn being anything but Platonic, or any justification for Evelyn's warning her against the danger of physical attraction. (Nor was his wife in need of the *Instructions Œconomique*.) Evelyn at fifty-two apparently considered himself qualified to incite it, or to put it to the test. At least he must have warned her. This seems to be her reply : ' When cheap thoughts arise of you I believe I shall pay dearly for it, for I must undervalu that which I have often upon my knees acknowledgd as a blessing : but why will you say thes things ? ' Unsophisticated as she was, such a risk had simply not occurred to her. But it is doubtful whether the naïve innocence implicit in her question went home to him.

Some of the first fruits of that immense labour Evelyn expended upon writing various devotional offices and meditations were acknowledged in this letter ; first efforts which were not it seems wholly praised by her : ' thus I begin ', she says, ' to giv you an account of your booke : the Christ mysticall and the medetation patheticall are t[w]o very good things, that is here and there a litle . . . if you would bestow a hour or t[w]o after your bread and wine of a friday or a saterday night to look it over and colect, I thinke it would be a good incitement to medetation at any time, and might itself begin one of the weekly on[e]s you are making : for there is nothing so worthy our thoughts as the love of christ to us, and our real

relation to him in all perticulers : this is at your plesuer
to be performd and but humbly offerd, not at all urged
upon you : for your caer to improve my knowledg in
toungus [tongues] I render you humble and hartey
thanks : we will talk about it when we meet, you shall
hear what I have to say upon it : about spending time
I have mouch to say : I will be at church on tusday, or
if you could hold it lawfull to com to St. Jeames Chaple
to prayers, I shold be glad, becaus Whithall is very late
you know becaus of the king, and my lord Berkeley gos
(now he is not well) to dinner early : your prayer is
exelent : your motto good and prity : your grammar
shall be stitched : for all you laugh I love a good plain
honest leter : god keep you.'

Her instruction in foreign languages probably made
little progress ; at least there is no other reference to
them throughout their friendship. In any case, her
words, ' You shall hear what I have to say upon it ',
imply some hesitation in adopting his suggestion.
' Spending time ' is perhaps her phrase for the charitable visits to the sick and the poor they often made
together.

What are we to infer from her words, ' for all you
laugh I love a good plain honest leter ' ? In writing to
her, Evelyn adopted in his one or two surviving letters,
a particularly florid style of which Margaret did not
entirely approve. Does she not give him a hint as to
the ' good plain honest ' style she prefers, when she
writes : ' your prayer is exelent : your motto [1] good
and prity : your grammar shall be stitched ' ?

Now this first letter impels an important question :
Why should Evelyn say that the letter giving her

[1] *Un Dieu un Amy*, see p. 41.

thoughts on the compact was received ' a little after '
the signing ? By Margaret's reference to Lord Berkeley,
it could not have been written before 8th January 1673,
when she moved from Whitehall to Berkeley House.
Therefore we have no surviving word from Margaret's
own hand before 8th January. Furthermore, is it not
strange that no other letters do exist between 16th
October 1672 and 8th January 1673, and that no
meetings immediately subsequent to the pact are
recorded in the *Diary* until January 1673 ? Of course
they met in this period ; the subject-matter of this first
letter puts it beyond doubt. Immediately following the
extracts from the letter given by Evelyn in the *Life* he
places his account of the changing state of the relationship between Margaret and Godolphin. But this crisis
apparently had its origin in Godolphin's illness when
he was in France in the summer of 1672, and reached its
climax in the signing of the pact in October. Godolphin
was well enough to cross the Channel in October, and
by the end of the year practically fit and staying with
Lord Arlington at Goring House — which was on the
site of the present Arlington Street. Perhaps no
other letters survive because their subject-matter was
too delicate : the responsibility for the change in
Margaret's relations with Godolphin may have been too
apparent. Evelyn, conscious of the gap in the narrative,
is forced to reduce what was, in fact, three months, to
' a little after '. There is, however, evidence of Evelyn's
share in the change of Margaret's attitude towards her
lover Godolphin — of her modulation from secular into
sacred love — either at the time of the pact, or very soon
afterwards. In the weeks following the pact, and before
Christmas, 1672, Evelyn wrote an *Office for Nativity* for

Margaret's own use; which is the earliest surviving devotional office written by him for her. It is in a shortened form of many others based, in style, on similar works by Jeremy Taylor, Symon Patrick, and Henry Vaughan [1] that he subsequently wrote for her, comprising a psalm, a meditation, and a benediction. In the meditation, Evelyn put these words into Margaret's mouth : ' Ah, is it true indeede, that my God will dwell on Earth, whom the heaven & heaven of heavens cannot containe ? Is it true indeede that my Saviour has thus loved me, loved me better than his life ? How is it that not the mother of my Lord, but my Lord himself is come to visite me this day, and to vouchsafe to invite me to him ? Haile ô Incarnate Word ! I adore, I admire, I prayse, I magnifie Thee, yea I love thee, for thou has loved mee, when I loved thee not, when I loved the world, and the follys of it ; and art come to mee, when I sought thee not ; to dwell with mee when I was abandon'd & desolate, and knew thee not . . . come, take possession, dwell in me forever ; say, this is my habitation, here shall be my rest, for I have a delight therein. . . .

' Ah, how I tremble when I but think of my fraility, or that for my sinns, thou shoud'st leave me to my selfe : Lord, I entirely depend on thy power, and goodnesse, to preserve me from ruine : never leave me, nor forsake mee ; for the more I consider the dignity, the more dear Lord, I dread to fall from it : O let me be ever low in my owne esteeme, that I may be high in thine ; let my Ambition be to serve thee, my delight to obey thee, my Glory to admire thee, and never to set my love upon any Creature, which may take it off

---

[1] E.g. *The Mount of Olives : or solitary devotions*, 1652.

from thee : What ever pride thou seest remain in me, inable me to conquer, to leade it in triumph, to trample on myselfe, chaine it to thy Chariot, and drag it after thy Crosse . . . consecrate my Body, clense my thoughts, prepare my Heart, purifie my Actions . . . that thou mayst not only be this day borne anew in mee, but find a new place, and dwell in me forever. . . .'

Here we may see the hidden pill in the jam in the words ' never to set my love upon any creature ' with their denial of human affection. Here lay the discrepancy between Evelyn and Vaughan, the latter going no further than ' certainly it is dangerous medling with the world '. We see, also, the discrepancy between Evelyn's actual attitude and his words in the *Life*. So we have some justification for our lack of faith in his words : ' I had oppos'd a melancholy Resolution she now and then Entertain'd me with of absolutely Renouncing the thoughts of Marriage.'[1] This submission to Evelyn's will doubtless formed the subject-matter of their meetings and letters between October and Christmas ; but no letters survive and no meetings are recorded. Doubtless the time was absorbedly spent and passed quickly. But not so quickly for Mrs. Evelyn. We must remember, however, that the journey from Deptford to Evelyn's lodgings in Whitehall could be, at this time of the year, tedious by coach and dangerous by water ; therefore his habit of spending more time in London on business than he spent at home with his wife was justifiable. But between the signing of the pact on 16th October and the 21st December Evelyn spent fourteen days with his wife and forty-five in London.

[1] *Life*, pp. 31-2.

It is not at all unlikely that Mrs. Evelyn now regretted her encouragement, at the outset, of his friendship for Margaret ; his absences from home were becoming more frequent and more extended in duration. On the 28th November he went to London, and we might well be persuaded by the entries in the *Diary*, that he spent the time in a normal manner : he was chosen Secretary of the Royal Society, heard three sermons and received the Holy Communion once, solicited money at the Treasury for the sick prisoners, attended the Council of Plantations, supped with Lady Sunderland, and carried out some public business. There are, however, in the *Diary*, several days in this period left blank. What he was doing we can only surmise.

Mrs. Evelyn, tired of stilling and preserving, and with no one more exciting to talk to than an occasional sailor from the Deptford Naval Yard, felt somewhat neglected. And it would be Christmas in five days. Exercising her ingenious way of using expressions very pleasing yet somewhat obscure, on 20th December she reminded Evelyn of the difference between his courtly life and the quietude of the country ; and to bring home to him that she was a neglected unfortunate rustic she made a brilliant choice of the name *Hortensia* :

' D Philaretes   from Philyria
   ' I hope you do not imagine though I live in the Countrie and converse with sea Nimphs, now and then with a Tar-pauline Hero, that I do not aprehend the difference betweene this kind of felicity, and that which you possesse in a glorious Court amongst great Beauties and witts, and those so refined that the charms of that splendor has no influence on their spirits, persons whose

Ideas are of a higher nature, whose minds are pure and actions innocent, these if I could be capable of envie, I should make the subject ; but I am so farr failling in that kind, that I rejoice in yr happinesse, I acknowledge you a better judge of such perfections, and to merit the honour of being an admirer of the Calme Beautifull and prudent Alcidonia, the friendship of the sprightly Saint, and to be allowed the liberty off a playfellow to Ornithia whose excellencies unites admiration and esteeme, since you have quallifications which entitle you to as much good fortune as any man, if knowledge and discernment in curious and choice speculations, joyned with virtues not common though desirable in yr sex may obtaine returnes of friendship from persons who cannot be unjust and therefore must allow you a share of their esteeme, you may pretend, but should I hope for a part, it must be upon no other account but as I have a litle interest in you and possibly am kindly thought of by you, which happinesse produces many advantages to Hortensia.'

In response to this charming and touching appeal, Philaretes (being a lover of virtue) returned home the next day.

CHAPTER IV

CONFLICT

1673

WITH the Deptford Christmas sermons and festivity over, Evelyn returned to London on the 31st December, in readiness to call on Margaret (who was slightly indisposed) the following morning and to wish her a happy new year. He took with him one of his written presents for her, a devotional work of eleven pages, entitled, *Circumcision or New-years-Day Office, A New-yeares-gift*, in which he incorporated for her utterance this further incitement to sacred love : ' Lord ! make me willing in this day of thy power, or rather that of thy Grace ; and this very day, in which I heare thy Voice, let me no longer harden my heart. It is *that* which thou has injoyn'd us to give thee ; ah take it dearest Lord, and make it worthy of thee : circumcise it from the flesh and clense it from its adherences ; Breake-up the fallow-ground, and let me no longer sow in thornes : wash it from wickedness, that I may be saved, and let vaine thoughts lodge no longer within me : Thou who lovest Truth in the inner parts, free me from all Hypocrisy : The Heart, O Lord, is deceitfull above all things, and the Imaginations of it onely evill, and that continualy : O sanctifie my Whole Man, Spirit, Soule and Body, and let me never fall from my Integrity.' Evidently, despite the pact, Margaret was not yet able to satisfy Evelyn that her break with Godolphin was complete.

Evelyn next visited Margaret (who was still in Whitehall) on the 5th January, and to commemorate their pact, presented her with a handsome turquoise locket [1] set with sixteen diamonds — a pretty thought, to remind her of the 16th October. The locket contained, or formed, a five-pointed star or pentacle [2] thus ✭, probably with the letters of the word ΑΓΑΠΑ between its five points.

Without the Greek word it became Evelyn's symbol for Margaret, and like the 'good and prity' motto *Un Dieu un Amy*, henceforth marked all things written for her ; the letters she wrote to Evelyn were also marked with the pentacle by him. It is, perhaps, significant, that ΑΓΑΠΑ (spiritual love) was little used, though it was doubtless chosen with the best intentions. As we watch the development of the friendship, we shall understand why the word was discarded.

Two days after receiving the locket, Margaret obtained permission from the King and Queen to leave the Court for the purpose — Evelyn says in the *Life* — ' of vacating entirely to religion and solitude '. But her departure was more likely to be a natural sequel to her break with Godolphin, and to further her new attachment ; moreover, embarrassment at Whitehall would

---

[1] Evelyn paid a jeweller £11 for it on 3rd January 1673.
[2] The pentacle was not wholly reserved for Margaret. Evelyn so marked at least two books bought by him during his travels abroad. He so signed a letter to Sir Richard Browne, giving his thoughts on the death of Charles I, on 29th January 1649. In a list of 29th April 1673, he uses it against five entries of sums paid during 1672 to the Surgeon and Deputy Commissioner at Rochester. It also appeared on a map Evelyn sent to Pepys in December 1681. The addition of the pentacle to the Altar of Friendship was probably made in January 1673.

be avoided. Lady Berkeley,[1] the middle-aged handsome
third wife of Lord Berkeley of Stratton (whose brother
married Godolphin's aunt), expedited the change by
offering accommodation to Margaret in the new and
spacious Berkeley House, where, if she found fewer
opportunities than in Whitehall for solitude (for Lady
Berkeley loved company) she might find more for
devotion.

And there was the additional advantage of being at a
greater distance from Whitehall — the place for which
Evelyn considered himself unfitted. He tells us that
their Majesties were ' both unwilling to part with such
a pearl ', and says : ' how dim the tapers burnt as she
pass'd the Ante-Chambers . . . verily, I had not seen
so universal a damp upon the spirits of every one that
knew her '. The next morning ' all her household-
stuff, besides a Bible and a bundle of Prayer-Books were
pack't-up ' ; there was a touching farewell scene
with Dorothy Howard ; and another with ranting
Nanny, who became the possessor of Margaret's pretty
chapel or oratory. Evelyn, jubilant at his friend's
removal, accompanied her to Berkeley House. Here,
in this new setting, could he enforce the bargain of
privileges, visits, and discourse as claimed by him in
their pact.

Berkeley House had been built by Hugh May the
architect soon after the Restoration. It cost Lord
Berkeley thirty thousand pounds and was one of the
finest London houses, with porticoes in the Palladian
style — though Evelyn criticized its inconveniently
large rooms. The house and gardens enveloped a
considerable part of what is now Mayfair, more or less

[1] Born 1639, died 1698.

covering the present sites of Berkeley Square to Devon-
shire House, and from Hay Hill to Charles Street.
Evelyn had a hand in the lay-out of the attractive,
undulating gardens, advising the planting of his favourite holly hedges on the terrace.

Berkeley House will always be associated with Evelyn
and Margaret — or *Electra* (the bright) as he now called
her, his visits to her room on the first floor going on
week after week with hardly a break for three years.
Her room with a roof of decorated plaster, approached
by a cedar staircase, was above the hall where the fine
tapestries depicting episodes in the life of Francis I
were hung. With Margaret established here, Evelyn
now began to record his visits to her in the *Diary*. He
also composed an anti-Godolphin prayer to inaugurate
their reading and praying together :

' For my ✶ Tuesday

' Ah, most Holy and deare Lord ! who hast promised
that where Two, or Three onely, are Assembled in thy
Name, there *Thou* wilt be : Let that gracious promise
of Thine be verify'd to us at this tyme : Humbly, we
come unto the Lord, or rather humbly Thou Vouch-
saf'st to come unto us ; and what are we Sinfull dust,
polluted Ashes ? . . . We are here prostrate before
Thee Lord, and now what do we beg of Thee, but that
Thou wilt give us thy-selfe : for earthly things we come
not (blessed be the goodnesse, thou hast prevented all
our Wants of them) but for Heavenly we seeke, for of
them we continualy stand in neede : We, thy poore
Creatures, devoted to thy Service, have solemnly
oblig'd our-selves to make Thee the onely object of our
happinesse, the tye of our mutual Friendship, and the
bond of our Christian Relation ; that as the Disciples

of the Holy Jesus, we may obey Thee to love one-another as thou hast commanded, in order to our Love of Thee, who so loved'st us, to give thy selfe for us : Deeply presse upon our hearts, and Affections this indearing Consideration : we seeke no other satisfaction, then that this Love of ours, may be totally iñers'd in the fruition, and Love of Thee : Ah, let that flaming Charity of Thine, which mooved Thee to do such great things for us (for what could'st thou do more than to dye for us ?) burne likewise in our Hearts, to consume all that is Earthy, and Sensual, and repugnant to thy Spirit of Holynesse. . . .' Again Evelyn insisted on the denial of human affection : ' Never oh never suffer us to depart from Thee O Lord ! for the Love of any Creature or Thing in this World — Our Frailties are many, our Temptations buisy, our Enemys mighty, and Snares are every-where about us : O let the Consideration of the danger, the experience of the emptinesse of all earthly contentments, the Eternity to come, and above all, the Sense of thy Love, carry-us-up, above the reach of this World, and never anymore to stoope to it againe : [1] . . .'

Tuesday, the day specially chosen for his weekly visit, sometimes proved inconvenient, but generally he dined, prayed, and read with Margaret four times a month. In the first excitements of settling-in, however, he called on her eight times during the January of 1673 — dining on one of these occasions with the Berkeleys, when Margaret may not have been present.

This initial frequency of visits perhaps explains the

[1] *An Eucharisticall Office*, p. 185. Written originally for Evelyn's own use. On being given to Margaret, an additional title, ' The Wedding Garment, or Trimming of the Lamp ', and a drawing of the Altar of Friendship was added to the title-page.

lack of letters in the period ; the second letter of the
year to survive being from Margaret, dated as received
by Evelyn on the 14th February (for she rarely dated —
or signed — any letter).   Under his guidance we see
that she is making the progress he desired.   If she had
any doubts about her break with Godolphin a few weeks
earlier, she has none, or few, now.   Evelyn's friendship,
possibly disinterested at the outset, cannot be said to be
so now.   We have seen a sample of the spiritual food
he gave her.   The form of his aspiration is apparent.
Not content with a friendship firmly based on religion
in the seventeenth-century fashion — in which her
interests would have been paramount, or at least equal
to his — he began to mould her into a spiritual toy or
plaything for the benefit of his own soul.   His love is no
longer disinterested.   He is blind to the needs of his
dearest friend, the object and inspiration of his devotion.
But she is not really happy, despite Evelyn's praise and
encouragement in her struggle towards celibacy ;   this
has bolstered up her estimation of herself, but she is still
sceptical of her own happiness : ' as for your letter ',
she says, ' 'tis very good, and givs me a good opinion of
my self, and that fuw [few] things do '.   Evidently
Evelyn praised her decision to renounce Godolphin,
and stated, in his own fashion, the religious grounds
that confirmed it : ' You must know ', she says, ' I had
resolved all this before, but not upon so good grounds
as now '.   His instructions have been given, and will be
obeyed.   She says : ' I doe not keep Lent : and doe entend
as near as I can, to doe all other things you speake of '.
      Where was nomadic Godolphin ?   What did he
think of the situation ?   Regrettably, he has left no
word.   Surely he and Margaret had met since his

arrival in England at the end of the previous October ?
Whether he was at Goring House, in Whitehall, or at
Newmarket with the King, news of Margaret's departure from Court, and of her friendship, would reach
his ears. We may surmise that Godolphin, on hearing
that Margaret was to leave the Court, made the first
brilliant move against the new friendship by arranging
with Lady Berkeley to provide accommodation and
to act as a *concierge* at Berkeley House — which was
but a stone's throw from Goring House. Evelyn
surely sensed the import of this move and the disturbing
proximity of Godolphin watching on the other side
of Piccadilly. We cannot but believe that he would
write to Margaret (and that she would destroy his
letters after reading them — as she destroyed all letters
from Evelyn). Whether they met, or whether he
wrote, he certainly watched, and lived up to the
King's delineation of his character ; he was like a
trout — stationary in the main current of a stream —
watching, backwards and sidewards, an elderly pike
entice a gudgeon into still and uncertain depths.

How long the enticement went on undisturbed we
cannot determine from Evelyn's *Life*. After describing
Margaret's arrival at Berkeley House, he says, ' it was
not long ' before she resumed her former inclinations to
' altogether abandon the world ', partly to avoid the
company that frequented Berkeley House and — he
goes on, making heavy weather of the explanation —
' interrupted her [devotional] Course, so partly, other
circumstances, that for the present, seem'd lesse favour-
able to her intentions of marriage so soone (and the dis-
quiet it put her to) '.[1] What do these laboured phrases

[1] *Op. cit.* pp. 38-9.

mean ?   Perhaps 'the other circumstances' may be
none other than her ties with Evelyn, which she hesi-
tated to break, and which he wished to retain.   But our
greater charge against him just now is that of confusing,
in the *Life*, the chronological sequence of events.
Immediately following his account of Margaret's
installation at Berkeley House, he gives the passage just
quoted, and goes on to relate a renewed conflict between
her love for God and her love for Godolphin, appending
the advice that he himself gave.[1]

The truth is, these events, instead of following her
arrival at Berkeley House, belong to 1674, and will be
dealt with in due course.   Therefore, apart from the
initial Berkeley House episode, not a word is given by
him regarding the interesting events of 1673.   And for
them we must return to the letters.   We may, perhaps,
discern some reason for Evelyn's omitting from the *Life*
any mention of the topics with which they deal.

Godolphin's movements after his return to England
in October 1672 are unknown, though it is probable that
he was domiciled at Goring House for the spring of 1673;
and he certainly made no new journey abroad until
June 1675.   An occasional meeting with Margaret may
therefore reasonably be assumed ;   in fact, whenever we
detect some failure on her part to satisfy the demands of
Evelyn, it is almost certain that Godolphin is in the
background, exercising his influence, perhaps meeting
her.   In fact, she began to realize that she was not so
spiritually attached to Evelyn as she had believed herself
to be ;   there were elements in her nature that would not
be content with his ideals.   Perhaps she had pondered
those terrible words : 'Never to set my love upon

---

[1] Pp. 39-48.

any creature', and in a feeling of revulsion slipped away occasionally to Goring House for a humanizing palliative. A few days before Easter 1673 something of the kind took place, Margaret eluding Evelyn ; in fact, she may have eluded him more than once, for in March he recorded only one visit — on the 4th.

For this affront, with typical mock-hypocrisy, Evelyn writes to her, blaming his own spiritual imperfections : ' I told you I was to go home this morning and would therefore have exchang'd a day with you ; but you were short with me, told me you din'd & suppt abroad, and slipt away like a fairy : *Electra*, it is not necessary, that I ever dine or sup with you againe ; but, I had a business to have imparted, and it would have detain'd you but very few minutes : That I reserve it till your better leasure, this paper brings you my excuse, if at least, I neede any : I know you can easily dispence with my little services for a longer time : since I find you continuing your later reservednes, your breathings after solitude, and perpetual complaints of the multitudes of your Acquaintance, which makes me feare you repent of having added one more to their number since October last, so much is *Electra* chang'd since she came into better ayre — The time will come when she will say — such — a person was my sincere Friend, faithfull, industrious, and without reproch : He was one I might with confidence have rely'd on, for he certainly lov'd me. I am sorry I made him no more sensible of my esteem : since I am sure, it was all he sought, and that such a friend, so unconcern'd, so intire, is not every bodys lot to find — This will make my Ashes some amends, when I am fall'n to them ; Well, there is a difference in good-natures, and great Witts

and greate Beautys are seldom guilty of much of that ;
Yet, there may be a *Phoenix* for any thing I know ; but
they say she is in Arabia and amongst the Spices, and it
is a greate way thither. Why was I so un-happy, or so
foolish to imagine that because I thought *Electra* the
Creature in the World, whom I would wish and choose
to be my friend, and the repository of my heart ; she
should have the same sentiments and opinion of me
unless our perfections had been equall ! This must
needes be the Cause *Electra*, of my ill successe, and I
acknowledge my injustice to you ; use me as you please
for it, only — allow me some share of your kindness ;
for the noblenes of the designe, and that I had so glorious
an ambition. Call me your friend ; for that's true, to
death I'le be that ; and be a little sorry, you can be no
more mine — because I am imperfect.'

Evelyn now makes a great effort — exciting in its
ambiguity — to reclaim her, knowing how near devotion is to love, and how melting, soft, and impressionable Margaret could be. ' But stay ', he goes on, ' is
there no punishment due to the little Thieves, who
steale away our hearts, give me that back againe if you
can. Now would this looke as like a love-letter as any
thing in the World, to any body living, who should
light upon it, but you & I : Nor without reason ; God-
Almighty knows my heart : I do love you ; but, it is
because you love Him : Whilst we both determine our
Affections there : we shall love each other, in the most
perfect fruition ; and if you love me there, and mention
me to Him with any peculiar Concerne you pay a just
debt, and I am satisfied ; for it is the top and sum of all
the Love and Friendship, which I will ever require of
you, or am capable of : My hearts desire is there, and I

do reckon much of my happyness from your constant Intercessions at that Throne, and, I assure you I have greate neede of them. I blesse God every-day for that Example of yours, which renders me better. . . . Let me never live a moment, if your piety, and the good which I both see, and every-day learne that you do, dos not tye my soule to you in our blessed Jesus.' He then compares her with the holy women mentioned by St. Paul : Phœbe, Aquila, Mary, Tryphosa, Julia, and Olympas, and concludes : ' Go on, blessed Saint, make more of your sex like yourselfe : The Lord is with you, and will reward your labour of love, and I will joyne my prayers and uttmost efforts, if at least they may be accepted : My longing is, that this may be the sole Object and End of our Love and Friendship : The dayes approach, in which we must do something Extra-ordinary (I meane the passion-weeke). Let us provoke one another, God allows the Emulation, and such a zeale as yours, not only pulls-downe his Blessings, but suspends his judgments, and sinfull Nations I am confident Subsist ; because your hands are lifted-up : Remember me in your Prayers, and *Let Brotherly Love Continue.*

' This is *Electra* a true Hieronimiticall Epistle (pardon the comparison) and I can shew you some more passionate betweene him and his *Devota Eustochium* : [1] You would think the old Heremite, realy in Love ; and so he was, but it was divine, and doubtless very holy ; and I assure you, I write of you, as I think : pardon my hast.'

[1] Eustochium and her mother Paula, fled from Rome to Bethlehem with St. Jerome. Extolling virginity, Eustochium founded a convent there : See Largent : *Life of St. Jerome,* 1900.

It is greatly to be regretted that these ' more passionate ' letters have not survived ; Margaret would destroy
them at once, and Evelyn's copies (if he made any)
survived only so long as it was discreet to keep them.

Margaret's answer, telegraphically brief, and pleasing
to Evelyn, soon came : ' You are my frind all is well I
se you are my frind and hartely and unfeignedly thinke
you so and ever did let me se you com in peace '.
Thus easily could Evelyn recall her by reaffirming the
ecstasy of his spiritual love, and so demonstrate the
Age-old pleasure of loving God, and of loving someone
who also loves Him.

The conjecture that Godolphin saw Margaret is
strengthened by Evelyn's ' reclaiming ' letter just
quoted, and the fact that she allowed Evelyn only one
visit in that month ; moreover, her next letter, written
soon after Good Friday, is sufficiently penitent to make
it practically certain that, on another occasion, she
strayed from Evelyn's fold : ' My dear dear frind,'
she writes, ' I love you from my soul : and so I will
always doe : whill I live and pray for you and whill I
live ever thinke myself your poor child : how great is
your zeal your humility your joy in the Lord and yet
you will make use of me his poor servant : to recount
the wounders of his love and joyn with you in praises
and so I will whill I live : my time myself and you my
friend are his and so we will be : today in the morning
I did likewis that penetenstial office that is I did deplore
my horid sins.'

The ' penetenstial ' office used by Margaret is one of
Evelyn's devotional works originally written for his
own use about the time of his marriage : its full title
shows its aptness for the present occasion : *Officium*

*Poenitentiae or Assistances in the Duties and Practise of
Repentance by Confessions and Deprecations with Prayers
and Devotions suitable to its Designe. To be sollemnly used
before our approach to the holy-Comunion and at all other
tymes of special Mortification.*

Margaret's contrition over her fall from grace is a
measure of her renewed obedience to Evelyn ; she
continues : ' Som fuw tears I had but all doe not deserve
like you : I had more then I could expect considering
my shameful neglect : after that I went to prayers, then
to the holy scripturs, then to diner, whilst your meat was
ashes and your drinke weeping and your wholl norish-
ment the doeing the will of god : after that I read to
my Lady Berkeley consarning the holy mystery : then
to prayers : then cam docter Benson [1] and I went to
confestion, and now I am writing to you : when I have
don, I will pray for you and this land and for my self :
the lord be gracious to us both and still may he refresh
your wearyed soul sens [since] it produces in you fruit
to his glory and your account : tomorrow I shall not
be at the first servis but will call you as I said and when
I said together we will pray : and when no longer you
will permit me, asunder : for methinks if I am but
with you I am safe. . . .' And then follows a sentence
which implies that she may well have seen Godolphin
for a week : ' How glad I was this morning to find holy
thoughts and quiet thoughts come to me after so long
a weeke of foly and madnes : on tusday a little before
six, nothing shall hinder us being together: but what doe
you mean by so litle a progres, what would you doe,
what [would] you be, oh lord you make my very hart

[1] George Benson, Dean of Hereford (*c.* 1614–92). Spiritual adviser to
Margaret.

LETTER FROM MARGARET BLAGGE TO JOHN EVELYN

ake to hear you say so, and I so very wicked : well I
hope to be beter. You need not thinke I shall not use
your prayer becaus it is not by itself : I love all that is
yours.' The lapse, whatever it was, is over, confessed,
forgiven, and all is as before.

Of course Evelyn derived the greater pleasure from
this spiritual attachment ; Margaret, young, melting,
inexperienced, became more agitated than pleased by
his protestations. In reply to what is probably one of
his ' more passionate ' letters, she writes on 20th April
(or thereabouts) 1673 : ' What mean you to make me
weepe and to break my heart by your *love* to me ? take
me and all I have, give me but *your love*, my deare friend
tusday is longed for by me, and nights and days move
a tedious pace till I am near you ! ' Margaret then
praises Mrs. Evelyn who had made two rare cleavages
from rusticity, on the 15th and 17th April, to accompany Evelyn to Berkeley House. Evidently all went
well, and Margaret joyfully anticipated a return visit
to Sayes Court at Mrs. Evelyn's invitation : ' Truly her
kindnes gives an addition of joy which I must tell you
is the greatest thing I can say, for whenever I reade your
leters, say your prayers, or look upon any of the infallible
proofs of *your love*, I can hardly have an increas of satisfaction : and yet indeed she rejoices me : we must wait
gods time, but I wish it were come with all my heart
and soule, for never was any *creature tyd to another in such
bonds of frindship* as is my heart to you, I am sure if I
do you som good, you are the instrument of all mine.'

The subject of Margaret's marriage is never out of
Evelyn's mind ; and her recent absence appears to have
prompted a question, perhaps as to a possible decision.
She is obscure : ' Who would you have me after whose

E

advice would you have me take,' she replies. She then adds a sentence, which confirms all that Evelyn's devotional writings have implied : ' *Your* as for my being marryed, you know you won't let me resolve '. Now all is as clear as daylight ; Evelyn does not wish her to marry, but desires to retain her for himself : thus his brotherly love is akin to persecution. The subject of marriage, however, is at present distasteful to her ; so she breaks off abruptly, with : ' There is enough of this, now to God again ', showing that not only is she anxious to drop the subject, but eager to speak of spiritual things and to please Evelyn by referring to his ' reclaiming ' letter : ' This very day did I read and dearly love that text in your epistle touching brotherly love. I tasted when I read, but did not think it would have ben so tenderly applyd to me this day : *may our love last as life* and *if there be a love to you or me when we see the god of Love*, oh may you be my companion in those bless'd aboads, wher we shall without any imperfection serve our *perfect* lord, amen with all my heart to your last prayer and may we be accepted.' Margaret concludes the letter by sending her service to Mrs. Evelyn and her blessing to Elizabeth, Evelyn's six-year-old daughter, who is to stay with Margaret for a few days.

With Whitsuntide at hand, Evelyn prepared another present for Margaret : the *Office for Pentecost*, or *Descent of the Holy Spirit*. Again he cannot refrain from inserting a few sentences to keep her to the celibate path, apparently ignoring the assurances of her last letter : ' Descend this day with thy divine Word into my heart, for the reformation of my life, and into the Sacred Mysteries, to communicate Grace for the sanctifying of

my Nature ; that I may spiritualy eate and drink the
Flesh and Blood of my deare Lord, and be enabled to
discerne his body ; for though he was manifested in the
Flesh, he was justified in the Spirit, and being received
up to Glory, will likewise Glorifie and bless us with all
Spiritual Blessings in heavenly places. Thither let the
desire of my heart ascend, and never come down againe
to dwell upon any-thing here ; for there is my Treasure,
and there, let my heart be also ; for thou Lord art my
hope, and the blisse which I long for. . . . I feele the
flames of thy Love consuming all my Affections to the
things below, and irresistably drawing me up unto
thee : Thou camest indeede to send fire on Earth, and
what wilt thou, if already it be kindled ? It is, it is
kindled O my Lord ! and from my Soule I desire to
feele the Warmth, to enjoy the Influence, and to walk
forever in the Light thereof : Burne-up, O divine Fire !
all the drosse, and refine the impurities of my Corrupted
nature. . . .' Again, the words ' never to dwell upon
anything here ' indicate Evelyn's desire to keep Godolphin out of her thoughts.

On 3rd May Evelyn first met Godolphin, when they
dined with John Hervey, the Queen's treasurer. Osten-
sibly, Evelyn desired to expedite the King's customary
gift of £2000 (now four months overdue) to Margaret
as a retired Maid of Honour ; perhaps Godolphin was
present in support. Evelyn would be glad of this
opportunity to meet Margaret's patient lover, and
doubtless Godolphin wanted to see her devout and
scholarly friend. All we learn about Godolphin from
Evelyn's *Life* is that he is ' an excellent person '. We
shall see, presently, the excellences of one who also had a
passion for gaming, and who indulged it to save himself

the trouble of conversation. Doubtless, as a good card-player, Godolphin mentally summed-up his rival, and said little. Margaret was aware of the meeting — and uncertain where her heart lay : ' I desire to se you on Wednesday to hear what succes you have had, and to tell what we have learnt of Harvey : in hast to goe to church I am yours with all my hårt ånd soul god blese you '. The Treasury were in no hurry to pay the money, and some months later Evelyn was again soliciting for it.

An entry in the *Diary* under 21st May 1673, recording Evelyn's hospitality at Sayes Court to seven guests including the Berkeleys, Margaret, and Godolphin, encourages us to assume that Godolphin (probably present at Margaret's suggestion) would lose no opportunity of taking Lady Berkeley aside, and with innate finesse glean from her something of Evelyn's weekly visits to Berkeley House. At least Godolphin cultivated her friendship, keeping in view her key position. Or we might believe that, now the lovers were together in public after so long a separation, they had permanently resumed association. For this latter belief there are, however, no grounds.

MRS. EVELYN
From a print after the engraving by Nanteuil

CHAPTER V

INDECISION

1673

FOUR weeks later, Evelyn, desiring a portrait of Margaret, persuaded her to sit and be painted by Matthew Dixon. Evelyn wished to pay the artist, but Margaret insisted it should be her present. On or about 14th June she writes to Evelyn : 'Dear friend I can but just tell you I cant live at this rate, to be always oblidgd and never able to pay you, but by loving you, and even for that I must be oblidgd to you for your beleev, for I only say it, never doe any thing but talke : but now if you will except [accept] it, I will set for your pictuer : a most rediculous present, but 'tis at your servis when you pleys : I will send to that man to get a cloth ready, and on Friday you shall go with me to set for it and tell how you will have it drest. pray let me se you, for I long for the day The Lord bless you and keep you and me.' Evelyn duly accompanied her to Dixon's place on 17th June, where a pretty scene was enacted. Apparently Evelyn, in his ' dressing ' the picture, suggested that Margaret's hair-ribbon would be better removed, whereupon the fifty-three-years-old gallant tied it around his wrist, and forgetting all about it, returned, with his wrist so adorned, to his Whitehall lodgings. On the following day, he wrote this letter — an essay on *obligation* :

' Truly, 'till I came up into my Chamber (after I left

y^u ' ye last night) and was kneeling downe to blesse you
(as I never faile to do, for all yr kindnesses to me) I did
not know I had ben a Thiefe ; but then I espied it about
my wrist, where it seems I had wantonly ty'd it : I
aske yr pardon, and I hope you will send it me, together
with your permission that I may waite on you to ye
painters on Thursday morning, that as I have seen the
beginning, so I may ye progresse and perfection of what
he is about ; and because every stroke of his pencil
concernes me ; pray deare friend, do not refuse me
this favour. I'le not faile to call on you at the house,
therefore, do not prevent me — I am, I confess, in
paine, and my heart akes at it, when I consider to what
trouble I have put you ; but, most of all, for having
nothing in prospect to recompense it, but you will have
it so ; God knows my soule, against my will and inten-
tion utterly : Why will you tryanize yr best friend ?
must nobody pretend to oblige you, without being
oppressed ? Would you have more of my heart, than
you have ? Well, if God hears the prayers of siñers be
assur'd you shall feele what you have don ; it dos realy
afflict me, and yet, rather then not be possessed of the
Treasure, I am so selfish, that I would still accept it,
though after your own way, and as you prevent me ;
but, upon my word, not as I desire, or did in the least
intend it : for, my deare friend, I seeke you, not yours ;
and yr patience in sitting, and above all yr permission
of so peculiar an honour, was the very top of my inten-
tion : But you are hard to me, in being kind, and I do
not deserve this usage : Reverse then this mark of yr
too generous nature, or tell me sincerely how I may
pacifie my selfe for having don you so little service for
so greate a reward : I could be vext at you, and with

my selfe for giving you this temptation, and yet, I have
no mind you should be angry, or repent, or think me
un-worthy, though I am so : do what you will with
me then deare friend, so you love me still, and abate
nothing of yr prayers to God for me, which is yet a far
greater obligation ; for that is *Substance*, this *Shadow*,
and it, and all the World must passe, God only remaines
forever, in whom alone there is no shadow of change :
I will more and more beseech that God to blesse you,
and some way or other enable me, to make you sensible
that he dos accept of my prayers for you ; It shall cost
me deare, but I will obtain that grace, and I am resolv'd
never whilst I live to cast my eyes upon that Image,
without a pure ejaculation in your behalfe ; and if you
think the reason why I so earnestly desir'd it, to be the
putting me in mind of our holy friendship, yr worthy
conversation, and to make me more religious, you think
that which is *True* upon my word : Upon this account,
I am content to allow of Images, and historical repre-
sentations ; especially, if resembling the persons, and
when the Meditation can be abstracted, and without
superstition. — My best friend, pardon this least grate-
full returne I can yet make you.'

The portrait did not please Evelyn — and it is not
difficult to see why : Dixon failed to portray any
sparkle. Perhaps any such expression was ruled out by
Margaret's posture and choice (if ' dressing ' excludes
the paraphernalia) of a tombstone for seat, and a funeral
urn for background. Perhaps Evelyn now regretted
tying back her Courtly curls. However, it was Margaret's present, and Evelyn could not easily refuse it —
even if unsatisfactory. Then Margaret suggested that
if Evelyn agreed, it could be given to Dr. Benson — but

only on condition that Evelyn made up his mind to like it. ' Non shall have the pictuer ', she says, ' but your self, unles you permit doctor Benson, but not him except you freely like it.'

Evelyn's essay on obligation in his letter of 18th June incurred Margaret's displeasure — as well it might — and she is pretty sharp with him : ' as to what you say of obligation I have no patiance to writ[e], and why you shold use such an expression after thos that have pasd between us I wounder : pray giv it over quite and for ever : I know the pleasuer I take in satisfying you to[o] well to expect any other payment without extortion.' She has no confidence, however, that her reproof will effect any alteration in his manner of writing to her ; she realizes that he is incorrigible : ' therefore forget the word or only let me use it, though I beleev you will not : for the same reason I forbid you '. She is obviously weary, too, of Evelyn's insistent habit of praising her for all his spiritual benefits : ' that you are beter I beleev it from my very soul, but I will tell you from whence it coms, and 'tis your own reason or els I shold pretend to giv it so confidently : you have endeaverd with all the sincerety imaginable to make me beter, and as you have said to me the more good one dos, the more tender one grows, and god is beter pleysd with us, and then we need [not] dout but we are beter : this is it and nothing els, therefore giv god the prais that you have so mouch grace : and for me I beg you will not yet so mouch prais god for me, as pray to him '. Margaret now becomes confessional : ' this I beg for I am yet bad very bad ', another indication that Godolphin (never out of the way) has succeeded, if only temporarily, in bringing her thoughts round to the

possibility of marriage.   Whenever she despises herself,
it is fairly certain that she has seen Godolphin, or she
has neglected her devotions in thinking of him.   At least
something has happened serious enough to make a
break with Evelyn possible.   She goes on, regarding her
' badness ' : ' I know it and you shall to[o] when we
meet if ever we doe '.   Actually, in July they met only
twice — as recorded in the *Diary*.   On 8th July he
visited her at Berkeley House, and in the afternoon went
with her and Lady Berkeley in the Duchess of Albe-
marle's coach to Twickenham, to call on Mrs. Talbot
(formerly a Maid of Honour and perhaps a friend of
Margaret).   Evelyn gives us no hint as to Margaret's
whereabouts for the rest of the month, nor do any other
letters survive in this period.   On the 25th July he
visited Lord Clifford, recently Lord Treasurer, at
Tunbridge Wells, staying five days.   For a part of
August Margaret certainly stayed at Lord Berkeley's
place Twickenham Park, to which Evelyn accompanied her on 26th August, stayed two days with her,
and returned home by himself.   Before leaving for
Twickenham, Evelyn gave Margaret another expensive
present, paying on this day no less than ten pounds
for a book.   We can only guess that it was some devotional work, sumptuously bound in his favourite red
leather.

   If Margaret and Godolphin met during this summer,
it would be at Twickenham.   Perhaps, however, she
needed solitude like Sir Francis Bacon, who, resting from
his own troubles, wrote there in 1596 : ' One day
draweth on another, and I am well pleased in my being
here, for me thinks solitariness collecteth the mind as
shutting the eyes do the sight '.   Perhaps it was not

solitude but Godolphin she wanted : if she met him there, she would find comfort in his calm and easy manner, as they talked together under Bacon's alder trees, or watched the placid swans gliding on the river. Not for nothing did Donne call it 'Twicknam Garden'.

And not for nothing would Godolphin pass the summer days with Margaret. Would he not divine that she was not wholly happy with Evelyn, and that Evelyn's possessiveness, almost against her will, had reinforced her love for himself? Would he not discern that Margaret was no longer the immature Maid of Honour, but that she had grown, out of her new spiritual experience, fully into womanhood with her love magnified, enriched ?

> Or if then thou gavest mee all,
> All was but All, which thou hadst then ;
> But if in thy heart, since, there be or shall,
> New love created bee, by other men,
> Which have their stocks intire, and can in teares,
> In sighs, in oathes, and letters outbid mee,
> This new love may beget new feares,
> For, this love was not vowed by thee.
> And yet it was, thy gift being generall,
> The ground, thy heart is mine, what ever shall
> Grow there, deare, I should have it all.[1]

So serious is the possibility of Godolphin having all her love, and of ending Evelyn's friendship, that Margaret strives to cheer Evelyn by recalling the great benefits she has derived from it : ' You have not known me long 'tis true, but I protest for all the treasures of the world I would not but have known you : not as other people, who wish it to hear you talke of trees and

---

[1] Donne : *Lovers infinitenesse.*

plants, secrets in natuer : and discours with you that
they may the beter entertain others : but I love to hear
you becaus often 'tis of god — to se you becaus it puts
me in mind of the joy the primative christians tooke in
seing one another : to read you becaus I often melt into
tears out of a sens of your vertu and my own — what
shall I call it wretchednes, wickednes, foly, every thing
that is ill : I love you for god and som times I thinke
I love god for you : you know how I mean : you often
com into my mouth in my prayers, in my thanksgivings
for your example : in my confestions that I make no
beter use of what I have reseaved from you : in my
petistions that I may be like you, and in my intersestions
— what thinke you are left out ? no you are often the
first : always the second, that is after one : and somtims
both together.'

So Godolphin is first in her prayers. Yet, at present,
though he is obviously very often in her thoughts, she
regards her attitude towards him as folly : in spirit she
is still attached to Evelyn : ' Endeed I love you and what
I have at any tim promisd you, if it lye in my power, I
will perform — I daer say I may promis again — for
you will never aske anything but for my good : by you
I will be derected '. Yet we must not overlook her
' I daer say ' and ' if it lys in my power ', naïve tricks of
qualification. ' By you I will be derected ' is plain
enough ; she will not marry without Evelyn's advice
or consent. She continues : ' I relye upon god and
from my hart I wish that his unerring will may ever
be obeyed : I have reason to say I am his when he will
permit me to call him min : I will not se to[o] far in
this world but looke upe above it, and ther I know you
will not leav me . . . your leters are not troblesom :

my awnser is surley becaus I don't like you shold beleev or mistrust they can be so : I minded very well what I said, and will not recall my words but will at any tim act what I have writ : ' qualifying again with ' if it lys in my power . . . I will writ and pray : but you shall rest a whill, and when your evening thoughts are good I would but you shall rest.' With an air of resignation, she finishes the letter. ' The pictuer is yours when and as you pleys : may you and yours be always under the shadow of the Almighty : and yet may his face shin upon you.' Within a week Evelyn had bought a frame — costing £3 : 5s. — for the portrait, and bravely hung it in the bed chamber at Sayes Court.

Mrs. Evelyn's adoring correspondent, her brother-in-law William Glanvill, to whom she sent the news of Evelyn's ' seraphic ' friendship and the hanging of the new portrait, illustrated his disbelief in ' seraphic love ' and criticized Margaret's posture : ' Were I in love with you I could not love you better than I do, and since I am so perfectly your friend, I hope you will value me no less than if I were a passionate lover ; Because there is no such thing upon earth as seraphick love . . . I dare not wish our friendship had begun when we first saw one another, for I am conscious I could not have trusted myself with loving you twenty years ago [1] as well as I do now ; you in those days might have been safe in your virtue, but I could not then be sure of my peace . . . my picture drawn by Dixon might hang as well in the closet, as the lady's doth in the bed chamber . . . but I would presume, however, to fix mine eyes where I had bestow'd my heart, and not be drawn with dejected looks . . .' [2] Two months later

---

[1] His wife, Jane Evelyn, d. 1651.   [2] Letter, 21st August 1673.

Engraved by W. Humphreys

MARGARET BLAGGE
From a print after the portrait by Matthew Dixon

the portrait had become an embarrassment, and was transferred to the parlour.[1]

As already suggested, Margaret probably spent the greater part of July at Twickenham ; she was certainly there for a few days at the latter end of August. At the beginning of September she dined with the Evelyns at Sayes Court, and thereafter, Evelyn's visits to Berkeley House resumed their former regularity.

Michaelmas Day could not be allowed to pass without another present for Margaret, and punctually on 29th September the Meditation for that day was completed, and given to her two days later. A new note is introduced at the end of the extract given : perhaps as a result of her intermittent yearning for Godolphin, Margaret had not been quite so amenable :

' To Thee therefore holy Father I flie for succour, to Thee I come for protection. . . . By the power of thine almighty Word (who art thy selfe the Angel of ye Covenant) let the chaynes of my Sinns, and the fetters by which Satan has so cruely bound us, fall-off from my Soule, that I may follow thee, whithersoever thou goest . . . teach me submission and to walke circumspectly before Thee . . . teach me humility : and the fall of the Evil, not to be high-minded but feare : let the number and strength of thy heavenly host, preserve me from my Ghostly enemys, and may the flaming Love of Seraphins kindle in my breast an ardent love of Thee and of all that are thine : make me of an hospitable, sweete and courteous disposition : for so have some had the honour to entertaine Angels ; and above all so innocent and meeke, that I never offend any of the least of thine. . . . '

[1] Letter, 20th October 1673, from Glanvill to Mrs. Evelyn.

About the first week of October, Margaret, in emulation of Evelyn, sent him her first attempts in the writing of Prayers and Meditations : ' I send you here my poor weake first fruits and those not half ripe : but 'tis fit that he who was the planter shold gather them when and as he sees fit, perhaps he will transplant: dig or dung about it . . . I told you ther were many words left out : many things often repeated, that it was the beginning and midle part of a meditation. . . .' She then breaks into self-deprecation, a result, perhaps, of her summer recess at Twickenham or another meeting with Godolphin : making reference to ' thos sins which has [*sic*] brought upon me a dulns [dullness] in medetation, a scarcity of tears, and a coldns [coldness] in prayer: and many imperfections : but I labour against my sins and from my hart detest them : and I prais god am in love with all his comands : and I hope I shall improve : in the mean time ther is a vertu to be exersied in which is patiance : that I hope I shall make use of, and by that means I shall gain experience, and experience hope of which I shall not be ashamed.' Here she seems to say that in time, with patience, and experience of her new ways, she will lose the present shame she feels for her transitory dullness and coldness. We might almost say that she can discern the benefits of earthly love. Godolphin, we surmise, is at hand ; and, indeed, Margaret saw Evelyn only once in the first fortnight of October.

The scarcity of letters between the two friends is continued, and the only other surviving October letter is a copy in Evelyn's hand of one from Margaret, dated ' October the happy month ', presumably an anniversary commemoration of their pact. This is the letter

from which Evelyn gave edited extracts in the *Life*,[1]
in the early part of the narrative immediately after the
Altar of Friendship scene, thus putting words into
Margaret's mouth twelve months before she uttered
them :

'It gos hard with me when all I can do will not
persuade you : you are never unsesonable, allways
welcome : you seldom (or indeed I may say for I think
it) never come but by your descours or example you
impart some spiritull gift : after this I must be worse
then a heathen man or a publican did I not love those of
the household of faith — truly all my delight is in the
excellence[es] that are in the earth, and in my opinion
many sons have don well, but *thou* exceled them all — I
must confesse when the symbol [2] was made, I did not
think of the great tye that was to be between us upon
that acount : but so soon as ever you did inrich me with
treasures, which next the holy Scripture I value : I
lookt upon you as another creature, and did resolve, if
I could, to endear yu to me [note the qualification,
'if I could'] : and did praise God for you, and as far as
the circumstance of my life would permit [another quali-
fication] I resolved to make you my pattern, that
you serve me with industry (sure you don't imagin that
I can be such a monster of ingratitude as not to acknowledge) and though it has never bin in my power to
give the like testimony of my love : yet you cant but
remember with what obedience I sacrificed to your
intreaty those papers,[3] which I [k]new at my very
heart I was ashamed of : and that I do not do more is
because I can not, and that you neede it not, my dearest

[1] P. 25.   [2] Of Friendship, 16th October 1672.
[3] Her attempts at writing Meditations.

frind permit me, and I hope it is not amis, since I say it
with reverence, to use the same expression to you that
holy david also did concerning the ark of God — if it
might do you any servis I would most cheerfully
forbid mine eyes to sleep, my eye lids to slumber, or
the temple of my head to take any rest till I had performd it — this is truth. . . .

'I understood something of the office of a friend
before I knew you — but after what you have don for
me I believe I shall need but little instruction, gratitude
joynd with the greate esteem I had before will be, I
believ, in this case as good masters as the parrable — I
shall never have more frinds, I believe — my advice
will never be of any use to you unles to serv you as an
act of humility, and though I know that can be all the
reason you will ever have to use it, you shall coīand it
freely : I shall be glad to signify anything to you to
reliev you too, for I know if I shold not argue every line
of this part of your letter, you would not think me
sincerly yours : I shall till death be a real friend to all
yours, though I could wish there were more disposition
in some, than there is to this last article : ceremony you
know is my avowd aversion, and they allways use me
with so much that I go away discontentd, but patience —
and of this no more *I beseech* you, you see how I think
I am with you, that thus I dare speak my mind. They
that give money to the poore give all things, 'tis your
owne expression, they *that are a friend are all things*, that
is my own expression.

'I still love you more and more I se you love me,
I still love you more and more, I see you love God,
this looks like as if I were mad, but I write to a friend,
ah that word, how pleasant ! as to your viseting of

Ladys truly, there are so few fit for you that I think of
all the obligations you have laid upon me, I should the
least thanke you for this : I know I am not worthy,
more then my neighbours, but I have a mind to be
better, and when you have the will in keeping 'tis your
own fault if it be not put to those practises you like :
you see I am not proud, realy I speake what I think :
would to God I had *not alltogether so much reason to be
humble,* an almes I gave, a psalm and a prayer I said, and I
hope I shall improve : more the next year than I have
this, or you will rise up in Judgement against me :
Oh *that I did love nothing but God and you* — well I hope
I shall forsake everything for him who forsook heavn
for my sinfull soul — you said a line or so would do,
but this is two or three hundred, I hope you will not
be weary. I have every day of my life different requests
to make to God, so that after I have performd your
morning devotion, which the lord bless you for, and
read my chapter, I kneele down and say a prayer
proper to those occasions : the Tuesdays prayer I
have sent you, *I hope you will not despise me I know* I
sometimes fear it : pray if you think it fit for me to say
on your behalf, let me have it againe before Tuesday
next, that I may before we meete, offer it up to God :
the Lord keepe you. I praise God for your right devotion : you are very humble to put in any of my poor
collection : all yours is ravishing, you love god one may
see in every line, and that is the way I like.'

In her prayer for Tuesday Margaret, uneasy in her
love for Godolphin, has caught the confessional manner:
   ' . . . I remember my vanity, and am afflicted for
my folly in making childish and foolish friendships :
wicked and sinfull acquaintance, for interest, for sin, for

F

idlenesse : ah Lord, how much hurt have I don my selfe and others ? but thou art gracious and long suffering. . . . I blesse thee for my dear friend — whom this day I shall see : Thou hast shown me thy loving kindnesse : Truely my lot is faln in a faire ground and I have a goodly heritage. Thou hast not onely pardon'd me, but endow'd me with a friend whom I prize above wealth, nothing is like unto it. . . .'

According to this letter, the friendship is now running fairly smoothly, though sensing Margaret's spiritual aloofness, Evelyn fears he is not always welcome at Berkeley House. But Margaret endeavours to reassure him. Her assurances, however, hardly carry conviction ; she is more ' wordy ' than usual. Her protestation : ' I shall till death be a real friend to all yours ' encircles, surprisingly, Evelyn's family, showing her love for him to be less personal. But the most significant sentence in the letter : ' Oh that I did love nothing but God and you ', carries an implication that loving something or somebody besides God and Evelyn, she loves Godolphin.

Evelyn, naturally observed the 16th October, too, recording in the *Diary* : ' Anniversary, I writ to a friend ', but Margaret undoubtedly destroyed the letter — according to custom. In addition to her prayer for Tuesday, there appears in Evelyn's copy of her book of Devotions (all with Evelyn's spelling) — ' A prayer for my Friend : Tuesday ', and is as follows : ' Ponder my words O Lord and consider my meditations. . . . I come to prayse thee, and to pray unto thee for John Evelyn my Friend : I give Glory to thee for his labours of love, Brotherly affection, Christian and sincere Friendship. For the sensible improvement I have received from him, by mutual endeavours to glorie Thee in all Holy Conversation and Godlinesse : The blessed Offices, wholesome counsell and instructions which out of love to my soule, and to assist my earnest breathings after Thee, he has furnished me with all : for the frequent prayers he still puts up in my behalfe ; and his cheerful ayde and care of my temporall concernes, and the many many instances of a most faithful friendship to me. . . . Thou knowest that for Thy sake alone it is, I love this thy servant : However, therefore (to avoyd offence) we may be interrupted from joyning together in personal addresses to Thee, who hast promised thy special presence, if but two or three assemble in thy name ; and therefore forbidest none ; Yet heare thou me O Lord for my absent Friend, and heare him likewise for thy Servant this day and houre and forever : For whilst he is thy Servant never will I forget or be unmindfull of him : Inable me if it be thy blessed pleasure, to do him some good ; O may thy Grace supply what is wanting in me : Heare me . . . that thou will pardon his sinnes, pitty his frailities sanctifie his purposes, perfect his holinesse, prepare him for thy Selfe and receive him to thy mercys, where O let me meete him, with all Thy Saints in glory everlasting Amen. Blesse his wife, children and whole family — contented with the condition to which thou shalt ordaine us. . . . Thro Jesus Christ our dearest Lord and Saviour.'

From November 1673 onwards Evelyn visited Margaret more frequently ; in fact his calls at Berkeley House during the winter averaged six a month, and the letters, perhaps as a result, are less plentiful.

The end of the year, then, is the end of the first act

in this struggle for Margaret. Evelyn has stated his case, and at moments appears to be winning. But, just at those moments, Margaret seems to respond to the calls of the world, as Godolphin, unseen and elusive, touches her heart, perhaps with new declarations of love, and recalls to her memory the happy past before the advent and influence of Evelyn. Godolphin, however, has no easy task ; Margaret is no longer the patient girl waiting for marriage, for Evelyn has given her another choice. She is as loyal to him and as undecided as ever. The year closes on a touching scene between Margaret and little Anne Berkeley,[1] described in a letter to Evelyn : an emphasis upon Margaret's love of holy things.

' I did believe you would injoy our Lord to yourself when I was gon and shut me out of the room, but not out of your prayers I daer say : your leter was good kind devout holy christian pious charitable, everything that was good, I folowed its derection as near as I could : today I was, as Mounday last, left to my self again all alone, and I had not the hart to leav my god for a foolish viset : well I had a little worke to doe and at 5 a cloke I laid by that, and walkt about deeply considering the priviledg of us christians, the hapenes we are inured to, the asistance we have, the easeynes of the way, the glory of the end, the love of our god, the peace we posses, the justice the mersey the grace of our lord : and being set down in a chair, repeating again to myself the former considartion and apliying it home to my self, I heard a knocking at the door which I was not very well pleysd at, but I went to se who it was : and who shold it be but little mis Berkeley : so I askt the child why she cam, she

---

[1] Anne Berkeley, only daughter of Lord and Lady Berkeley : married in 1681 Sir Dudley Cullum, Bt.

told me her maid was gon out and she was come to be with me : the former medetationss were fresh in my head, and I fell a talking to the child and asking her if she had learnt a splam [psalm] I taught her, and other good discours we had, till at last I spoke to her about the love of our saviour in dying for her: she fell a weeping most bitterly, so I kist her and desiered her to tell me why she cryed : she told me becaus her saviour was crusifyd : I protest I wept too, but it was for joy and most thankfull I was to god for her, so then I made her a litle prayer to say, and she can read my hand : then I askt her if she were afraid to dye : she told me yes, so I gav her a litle book to read consarning death: and went to my evening prayers, wher with tears, I did prais god that he was pleysd to recompence so largly my retierment with such heavenly blessings : afterwards I made a prayer for my self consarning her, and in it I mentioned thos words of our lord: it were beter a *millstone*: she told me presently without my asking in what chapter it was, so that I found she had taken notice of it. I [k]now I was hartely pleysd and so I hope you will be, oh prais lord with me, let us magnefy his nam together. dear frind I hope on tusday we shall again be good, and on this next sunday we shall be hapey : I hope you will always love and asist me, I will always pray for you and obey you

' the grace of our lord Jesus christ be with you amen.'

CHAPTER VI

THE CRISIS
1674

EARLY in the new year, Evelyn introduced a new feature into the Berkeley House meetings — the Mental Communion [1] or Spiritual Communion, an imaginary celebration of the Sacrament with his own additions and rubrics. The practice, first used by him during the Commonwealth when celebration of the Sacrament in public was prohibited and only safe in private, appears to have been rather short-lived at Berkeley House, only on 18th and 25th January 1674 is its use there recorded in the *Diary*. Evelyn says it ' serv'd her some times in her privat recesses, and now and then, too, I think, in the Church '.[2] Perhaps Margaret was too responsive when they both participated. 'Did not our hearts burn within yesterday ', she writes, ' and our very spirits glow whilst we were in Communion with Christ : how delightful it is, what relish it kept all the day, and even to this moment, and must we not be very careful that we loose it not this week.' It propagated further rapture : ' O what thoughts ', she continues, ' had I last night of the union of Saints, oh Christ, I wish I were able to communicat them to you, but they are very hard to expresse, for it is not an individual privilege or Grace but something like that of the soul and body when they are made

---

[1] There is another version in Evelyn's *Devotional Book* (ed. W. Frere, 1936).　　　　　　　　　　　　　　　[2] *Ibid.* p. 86.

pure and serene in temper.' The version of the Mental
Communion used by her opens with a long and florid
confession, better suited to the Duchess of Cleveland
and cattle of that sort (as Evelyn would say) than to the
accredited saint of the Court. Perhaps it was only
used when Evelyn considered she trangressed. At the
words 'This is my Body', Evelyn devised a rubric to
induce something of the theopathic saintliness of St.
Gertrude : [1] 'Here imagine you see Our Blessed
Saviour's action, with what love and sweetnesse, he bids
them call his future passion to mind, when he should be
absent from them, and you to his Feast.' And at ' This
is my Blood ' : ' Then imagining him reaching the holy
Elements to you '.

In the same letter, we see how sensitive she was to
Evelyn's more passionate outpourings : ' I have letters
of yours ', she says, ' which break my heart to pieces at
any time . . . and that . . . before Ye Communion,
and that divine ejaculation of yours before receiving ye
Sacrament O how heavenly are they, my dear friend, I
blesse you . . . indeed I love to see you, and be with
you, but nothing obliges me so much as when you write
to me . . . how much I wish you had time, and would
now and then surprise me, why not now and then with
one of your prayers . . . what does most affect you,
and so help your friend forwards. . . . Now my mind
is at rest for tonight. Send me those papers : I mean
ye Mental Communion.'

Whatever heights of rapture she attained in the early
months of 1674, it was obvious by April that she could
not live up to Evelyn's standard, and her mood again
changed to one of self-deprecation, as it had so often

[1] See W. James, *Varieties of Religious Experience*, 1925 ed., p. 345.

since last year's secular summer holiday at Twickenham.
As the winter letters are few, we must look elsewhere for
light on the transition ; and again we see that in the
unabated stream of Offices and meditations which
Evelyn wrote for her (practising longanimity himself),
he still considered it necessary to make his saintly friend
give utterance to several lines of spiritual abjection.
These appear — strangely enough — in *An Office for the
Lord's Day* (wherein is contained the Mental Communion) a closely written octavo volume of 169 pages,
in form somewhat in imitation of Henry Vaughan's
The Mount of Olives (1652), and completed on 15th
April 1674 :

' I am toss'd with the Tempest of my impetuous
passions, and disturb'd by every accident of life : O
Thou who commandest the winds to cease, and the
raging billows to be still — Rebuke the waves of my
unruely affections, cõmand a calme, and grant me that
peace which passes Understanding. I am stung and
bitten with the firy serpent of my sensual appetite . . .
raise my affections to nobler desires, pluck out those
tormenting darts and quench the ardours that consume
me . . . withdraw my affections from the perishing
things of this life, which are nothing but vanity and
vexation of spirit, and fix them on Thee. . . . But thou
wilt have us give it [my heart] thee ; and were it
worthy of thee, how willing would I be to part with it :
Indeede O Lord it is not worthy : But since it is thy
desire, and that so thou vouchsafest to condescend :
Take it, my sweet Jesus, take it : Never will I require
it of thee agen, but to make a new oblation of it to thee,
when thou hast made it worthy of thee : Nothing (my
Saviour) is there in this world, which so bitterly

aflicts me, as that I had not presented it thee sooner, and
Thou hadst ben my first Love, my onely Love. . . .'

By Easter, the January melting had hardened ;
perhaps Evelyn's prayer was justified : A few days
before Easter she wrote :

' my trusty and wellbeloved secratarey I am perfectly
well satisfyd with your letter and doe thanke you for it
very mouch, it has don me good and I hope it will
others, but god knows I dont dout but god will aboundantly reward the great pains you take to refresh the soul
of his poor servant: if a cupe of cold watter be rewarded,
what is ther in store for you who have drawn so mouch
watter from me : and shed so many tears for me to our
dear lord, who dos not let one drope pase unregarded
by : today I prayd earnestly for you and your dear wife
and good children the familey of the faithfull: . . . I have
bin today refreshd a litle, but not as in tims past I have
bin — but 'tis more then I deserve gods will be don :
on sunday I shall at linconsinne be at our great feast upon
our high and meritoreus sacrifice Jesus christ the lamb
slain from the begining of the world, I hope you will be
though at so great a distance, a real pertaker of that holy
entertainment which our gracious god prepaers for his
humble ons : my great request to god is at this time to
be freed from my great backwardnes to all holy
aproaches.' In her own way she again confesses that she
is not proof against the attractions of Godolphin : ' my
coldnes in holy dutys, and my being upon the least step
into the world apt to be insnard by its temptations,
caught with its folys : in my bed I am slothfull, at the
table intemperat, in my thoughts idle, in my discours
trifleing : on every side I am poluted and defiled : but
you will pray I hope my beloved frind for me and my

weakness, that god would inflam my love, rais my
desiers, ingage my afections, conform me perfectly to
that patern of all vertu the lord Jesus our Master : on
tusday I hope we shall meet : I would faign have us *pray
together* and *read together* and *viset the sicke together*, that so
if we have one guardion angel he may at one tim se his
charge so well imployd.'

Margaret's letters reveal little more than the devotional ebb and flow of her nature. General topics are
never discussed ; perhaps Evelyn discouraged them.
He gives her a reputation at Court for wit, but that
quality is missing in her surviving letters. If she was
intemperate at table, she must have overstepped the one
or two dishes which Evelyn tells us was her self-denying
limit. Doubtless to the great eaters of the seventeenth
century this amount of protein did seem somewhat
meagre, though to our lean and modern minds (and
probably to Margaret herself who spent so much time
upon her knees) it was ample. It is refreshing to come
upon a hint of the maternal, especially if we have any
sympathy for her association with Godolphin, in her
letter of 21st May 1674, on the occasion of Mrs. Evelyn's
entrusting her with the six years' old Elizabeth Evelyn
for a few days at Berkeley House :

' So many excuses from *you* to *me* for so small a
buisnes is very grivous to me : and I beseech you let me
never hear any such thing from you more, for I take it
very ill truly ; blese us all what a company [of] words
for trusting me with the prityest best child [1] for a litle
whill : till you can with conveansey reseive her endeed
I take it ill : you need not fear her eating flesh for she
told us she never eat any a nights : her super last night

[1] See also *Diary*, 20th May 1674.

was goosbery tart : her humer incomparable : naturaly good but made beter I believ by an accedent, for her maid having forgot her litle nightcap, she lay in a suit of my night cloths, which was no small satisfaction to her: today she is to se the tombs:[1] in the night being hot she thruw of the cloths which made her cough a litle, but I coverd her and thanke god she slept well : a thousand thanks to Mrs Evelyn that she will believ you enough to trust me with such a jewel : I am suer I pray to god that I may well discharg my trust and so god blese you both amen. On monday we go twitnam [Twickenham Park] so that on tusday I shall not se my frind, my Lady Berkeley having stayd this weeke in complacence to me.'

Therefore in the last week of May, Margaret left for Twickenham Park. It is not known whether Godolphin suggested this surprisingly early departure for a summer recess, but it is certain he was very much in her thoughts at Twickenham during the ensuing months. And now that we have arrived at the events of the summer, which were to prove momentous, we may pick up Evelyn's narrative in the *Life* [2] at the point where we left it to deal with the events of 1673.

From the time of her departure for Twickenham, Margaret is again beset with indecision, torn between her love for Godolphin and her love for God : so Evelyn says, but we know that this conflict had never really subsided since last July. The first observation (and reminder), as we compare the letters with Evelyn's narrative in the *Life*,[3] is on his faulty estimation of time : he says Margaret 'had not been long' in Berkeley House before she was beset by these conflicts. Actually,

---

[1] Perhaps in Westminster Abbey.   [2] P. 38.   [3] Pp. 38-9.

it was eighteen months. And we cannot but be struck by Evelyn's sudden change towards her : ever since the compact, he had insistently and continuously urged her physical isolation, and now, in June 1674, he appears to be willing to let her marry Godolphin, or perhaps, more strictly speaking, advises her to do so. Unfortunately, Margaret's letters leading up to this change, and quoted by Evelyn, have not been preserved ; we must, therefore, look a little closely into his words in the *Life*, and remember that when Margaret is speaking, the words are Evelyn's.

Is it not rather surprising to us that he says he has really been touched in the deepest sense to see the conflicts she underwent, between her love and her devotion ? ' How often has she told me ', he writes, ' she would abide as she was ! and then her pitty for him [Godolphin] that could not live in her absence, divided her afresh, and pierc't her to the Soule.' Then she would have ' topics . . . ready to divert his passion, and reason him into an indiff'rence for her ; when (of all things in the world) it was not indiff'rent to her that he should have lovd her lesse '. But, having such ' absolute Empire over her-selfe, and such potent inclynations, to make God and religion the Buisinesse of her life ; that . . . she was many times upon the brink of resolving to have nothing more of secular in her thoughts: she believed that I (who knew *love to be stronger than death*) would never be brought to approve this resolution. . . .' Although this may have been Margaret's belief, it hardly accords with what we have learnt of Evelyn's ideal of friendship. Following on this resolution, she had ' a yet farther design of going . . . to Hereford, and live by herselfe ' under the direction of Dr. George

Benson, her spiritual Father. Here she proposed to live
'in perfect freedom, without formes ; frugaly ; without contempt : conveniently, without pomp : at
distance from the bussle of the world : Where I shall
forget, and be forgott'n : be arbitresse of my owne
time, and serve God regularly . . . and when I do ever
alter my condition, do it with my friend's advice, who,
I am sure, will never persuade me, to alter a purpose so
reasonable and so just for one in my circumstances.' ¹

This Hereford plan was temporarily dropped.
Evelyn next quotes a letter in which she is again considering marriage : 'I know not what to determine :
Sometimes, I think one thing, sometimes another : one
day I fancy no life so pure as the un-married : another
day, I think it lesse exemplary ; and that the married
state has more opportunity of exercising works of
charity : and then againe, that 'tis full of solicitude and
worldlynesse : So as to what I shall do, I know not :
He can live without a wife willingly ; but, without me
he is not willing to live : so as if I do not marry, he is
not in danger of sin : But if I, or he, or both should
repent !' Asking for divine guidance, she goes on :
'I am in a *streit*, and know not what to choose : determine thou for me, blessed Lord !'

As the summer days lengthened, she became more
restless, more undecided. Her arduous day of prayer,
devised by Evelyn, told upon her ; the greater part of
the day she spent upon her knees or reading indoors.
Only occasionally did she enjoy the pleasant gardens of
Berkeley House. There were annoyances, too, when
her devotions were interrupted to assist Lady Berkeley
in the entertainment of company. Lack of fresh air and

¹ P. 40.

exercise began to undermine her health. Just before
leaving the devitalized atmosphere of Berkeley House
for the open sunlit spaces of Twickenham for her much
needed holiday, she wrote :

' I am very sorey for your distemper that it kept you
from church : but you were hartely prayd for by me :
and *reason* good, for you were the instruement of my
being bathed in tears : and from my soul I beg you may
never want the refrechment I by you have reseaved from
heaven twice yesterday : first at the holy table and after
that in the evening in the garden : wher being alone and
with your booke,[1] the beauty of the ground, and the
face of heaven : did I thanke god convey plesuers
endeed : and that is word I can giv to no one thing
on earth I [k]now, and no such joy ther is as to have
bin hartley sorey : I have considerd your leter with
asstonishment : that you shold take all that pains, use so
mouch caution, have that caer and tendernes for me.
what am I — god knows a miserable siner good for
nothing . . . alas what am I able to pleys you in ? I
cant find fault with you nor inform you nor edefy you :
and but that you condesend understand what you say :
and from whens all this but from your goodnes : your
charity I mean, for that is the vertu which I admir in you
and which has preferd me so near your hart : for first
you hope I am beter then I seem, and you beleev me
wiser then in appearance I am : and next if I were non
of all this : why, becaus of that you woud if posable
make me somthing : this will make me prode of you
but never of my self, ah lord help me, for every day I

---

[1] On 19th July 1674 Evelyn paid £1 : 6 : 6 for a book he gave her.
But Margaret may have alluded to the book of Devotions, *Officium
sanctae & individuae Trinitatis*, given to her by him.

have les reason then other to thinke well of myself, the
more I know myself, the les I like myself, and yet for the
treasuers of the world I would not but know my self :
and I pray I may doe so still more and more, till I com
to know even as I am known : I doe most hartely thanke
you for telling me of my looks, they are too grav but
'tis as you say plesent to my self, though not so to others,
and I never thinke les of the world then when they beleev
that look is put on, for them may be, for som judg
hardly of me : would I could as easely be freed from
my own faults of that natuer, as I can forgiv them
against my self : I will be suer to remember your fears
for me in the reading this booke, and next gods grace I
know nothing will keep me sooner from exstrava-
gancys [1] then griving you : who already have had but
so litle plesuer from me, for the troble I have given you,
and suer I shall not increas it . . . I hope you are not
weary.'

What a change Godolphin saw in Margaret when
she arrived at Twickenham Park ! What compassion
he felt for her ! Her nature, always impressionable,
melting, showed signs of breakdown ; the ascetic
denial of earthly delights showed in her face, now pale
and lean. Now her body could generate no love for
Godolphin without a disturbing spiritual upheaval. So
precarious was her condition that any attempt on his
part to fan the embers of her affection might have
endangered her mental stability. But in his wisdom
and evenness of temperament he could discern and
soothe.

She could not think on marriage for long without
remembering her obligations to God : ' so little able to

[1] Spending too much time at her devotions.

make Him any returne . . . the first moment I am
tried, I shrink away, and am passionatly fond of the
creature, and forgetfull of the Creator . . . most
bitterly have I wept, to think how much of my heart
he has, how litle, my B. Saviour, who has loved, and
suffered for me so much more'. So Margaret asks
Evelyn for advice. ' Now should I marry, and refuse
to go to my Lord : part unwillingly with him, when
another so graciously calls ; What, O what would
become of me ! No, no, I will remain my B. Saviours.
Hee shall be my love, my husband, my all : I will
keepe my virgin[ity], present it unto Christ, and not put
myselfe into the temptation of loving any thing in
competition with my God.'

To this Evelyn says : ' that with no small difficulty
I at last brought her to capitulate' (though we see little
capitulation), and proceeds to give us the substance of
his reply [1] to her request for advice. This *volte-face*
— probably written about the end of June — survives
in his very neat copy of a letter sent to her at Twickenham, and deserves to be given in full, for in the *Life*
he omitted, or paraphrased, considerable portions of it.

' I am oblig'd to believe your opposing my Advice
the other day was more to improve your faculty of
maintaining paradoxes and of making good whatever
part you undertook, than that *Electra* spoke her thoughts;
since it cannot be agreeable to her piety, nor to the
equity of the thing, that any lesse consideration, than a
prospect of inevitable ruin, should suspend her resolutions of giving herselfe to a worthy person, whose
approaches have ben so honourable, and where the love
is reciproque : There is nothing more productive of

[1] *Op. cit.*, pp. 43-5.

calamity, than where love (as they call it) makes the
Bargain and passion blinds the man ; but so the young-
things precipitate, the giddy are caught, and when the
fancy cooles, repentance succeedes, and it ends in aversion and anxiety : This, I confess is deplorable and sad ;
But these Calentures concerne not my *Electra*, nor the
person whom I wish happy ; for though inclinations
begin the Addresse, and Love promotes it ; she is of
Age to discerne, and of prudence to resolve, and it were
to be very impertinent to interpose and be officious,
where there is no neede of the zeale, and for which one
shall have no thanks :

' This is, *Electra* what I should well deserve, if in my
late discourse with you, I had so much as the least
temptation to be curious of yr concernes, and pry into
your intimacies farther than becomes a friend, though
your friend, and such a friend : I assure you he desires
it not, he dos not seeke it. But when all the world gives
you for *Bespoken* and that you went from Court to
consummate ; when all who know you approve of it,
and I (for whose Counsell you tell me, you have some
value) do so too ; it is not rudenes in me, to aske when
it will be, nor un-kind in you *to not* reveale the secret,
if you have a mind to make it on : But, when all things
else are moraly to be prosperous, that such a *set* of
circumstances as in *Idëa* you have form'd, must be more
than in prospect before you can allow of any felicity in
the conjugal estate ? 'tis *that* which I dislike *Electra*, and
as a friend, am oblig'd to reprove you for.

' It is not enough to say you can be happy alone, when
you can make another so too ; but neither are you to
render your selfe miserable, because another loves you,
for that were to betray you both, and to make it your

act ; nor on ye other hand ought you to resolve not to change condition, 'til you can set your Neast on high, and be out of the reach of Accidents : where is the *Mediocrity* you professe ? It becomes a cruell Laban to exact a double Apprenticeship for a *Rachel* and a *Lëa* : *Saule* put *David* to Adventures for a wife that reproch'd him : But the Heroic-times are past, and we proceede now by other methods : she, who with your prudence, cannot live hapily with a thousand pound a yeare, will live uneasily with three : I wish you *ten* and as I am a Christian, if it were in my power, I would divide my poore fortune with you, and settle it imediately upon you, with as much freedome, as ever I parted with six-pence ; that you might see, by no com̃on effects, that there is such a thing Friend in the world ; and if you do not heartily believe it, you injure me in the tenderest part, because you thinke me un-sincere.

' But, you object, there may be a multitude of children and there may be few, and perhaps none : If many, there is exercise for yr Faith, your Patience, Industry and other Graces : Happy is the man who has his quiver full of them : Do you make nothing of what the *Apostle* has sayd ? *She shall be saved by child-bearing* ? I tell you some have ben almost in despaire because they had none, and they, have for the most part, ben such, as feared they should have too many : I have often observ'd that those who repin'd lost them all, and with it fortune too, and such as rejoyc'd in their store, to be prosperous in both : There is not a greater argument of Distrust, than this, and you do not well consider it ; if you should have no children, you tell me you should be displeased too : In sum̃ you cannot be happy, unlesse you may be so alone, or appoint the numbers and set

downe the portions ; not minding that the few may be
fooles, or vicious, which is worse ; and that one of the
many may recompense all your cares for the rest : But
you will give no Hostages to Fortune ; If she who had
bore you had ben of your mind there had ben one lesse
Saint for Heaven, I had wanted the best friend in ye
world, and so would many others, who now blesse God,
for ye charities you do them.

' Where is then my Electra's humility, her Faith, and
her Love ? There is ten times more exercise of Vertue
in the Married condition than in the Coelibate, which is
for the most part affected, singular, morose, covetous,
obnoxious to temptation, and full of reproch : But to
be eternaly sick, and with child — It is better than ye
fitts of the Mother, without being one ; and there are
an host of infirmities, which I could enumerate, to
which old Mayds are subject : The paines of Bringing-
forth affright you : Little woemen have little difficultie
and thus injoy the bringing a man child ; Queenes have
gon into the world before you in it, and 'tis to serve
your Generation in the most necessary instance, endeares
you to yr Offspring, to your Husband, your Relations,
and the Comon-wealth ;

' I do not see that the most opulent Coupples are
exempted from Cares, we find the contrary, and that
men of lower fortunes, and lesse ambition live hapily
and with comfort : There is unexpressible contentments on the mutual affection, and society of worthy
marriages, I say nothing of sensual circumstances, which
fall short of our imaginations, and is trifling : Children
are extraordinary endearements : There is something of
Despotic and *Royal* in being Mistris of a well govern'd
family ; and you, who are so rarely furnish'd for it,

deserve the dominion : Do you esteeme it no honour to have given Saints to ye Church, and use-full members to ye State in which you live ? That you can be hospitable to strangers, Institute your Children, give Instruction to your Servants, example to your Neighbours, and be parent of a Thousand other Blessings ?

' Marry in Gods name, *Electra*, Marry, and be not over solicitous for the future ; but be provident and Discreete : Ayme not at ye Ease or pomp of living, but at a Mediocrity ; Your ordinary prudence with a sedulous piety will conduct you hapily to that port : but, if you will adventure nothing in the Lottery, because they are not all prizes, your Faith is weake, I will not say, what is else too strong ; and you cannot object, one syllable of what the Apostle produces upon the subject, because the Circumstances wholy differ, and the decency of this age permitts it not :

' Though if I would betray you (as perhaps I might) I could turne the Argument upon myself and shew you another face of things in the Reverse ! If I studied onely my owne satisfaction, I should rather promote this aversion in you, and seeke to fortifie your suspicions : For as I professe it, the greatest Contentment of my Life, that you have vow'd your Friendship so solemnly, and that you will be Constant ; whilst I incite you to marry, I indanger it to another ; perhaps your Husband may be jealous, though without cause, or he have aversions to me, or may not be noble and free and ingenious : or make you unhappy otherways, which were all-one, as if I my selfe were so ; and you may change your mind, and repent: wheras being single, you are Mistris of your selfe, and your Conversation and your Vertus, and my Yeares, and both our discretions will preserve the

Friendship honorable, pious, and use-full ; In a word I
have sayd nothing upon the other topick, but what I
could un-ravell with the glory of Virginity, the Ease
of a Single-life, the opportunities of doing more good,
of Serving God better, of prolonging life ; by Examples,
and precepts from Scripture and Fathers, from Legends
and Histories, and present you such a lovely picture of
that state, which (approching next the nature of Angels,
who neither marry, nor are given in Marriage) would bring
you to suspence indeede and make you cry out with the
Apostle (in no unapt comparison) *I am in a straight
betwixt two, and what I shall choose I know not* —

‘ But I spare my *Electra* ; nor needes she arguments
to render her more unkind to *Hymen*, and to the repose
of One whom she knows, & I pitty —

‘ This is *Electra* the product of my staying for
Mr Jones, for whom I have waited till almost night ;
but, I thanke him for it, if you pardon the freedome I
take to discourse thus with you, and that it dos not too
much interrupt your buised Soule, which justly takes
occasion to tell me of long visites, and yet permitts me
to make them, though, if I did not love her company
above all things in ye world, I could recount to her, and
that truely, that I have as many things to take up my
time, as any she can enumerate, and some hundreds
more of very laudable Employments : so as ’tis not for
want of something to do ; but because whilst I converse with *Electra*, I can do nothing better, and of more
advantage to me : There are those, it may be, would
love me as well, or at least, make me believe so : but
their reasoning is not material, nor their company
agreeable to my spirit, and I can never be divided, who
am wholly yours, and so resolve to live and dye.

' Your little favorite [1] is better I prayse God.'

This letter provides another instance of Evelyn's inaccurate chronology, being dated ' 27 February 1672/3 ' (that is, 1673 New Style) which is certainly wrong. But it is clear from Margaret's letters that these events took place in the summer of 1674. Perhaps Evelyn made this copy (which, unlike others, is fresh and very neatly written and savours of embellishment) for use in the first MS. version of the *Life* when his dating would not appear so incongruous to himself as it does to us, owing to the omission in the *Life*, of his passionate ' re-claiming ' letter which — as we have seen — was written at Easter 1673 — indeed his omission of all the events of 1673.

Immediately following his advice on marriage, Evelyn refers to Margaret's desire for a *retreat*, saying [2] ' I ever persuaded her against the recesse ', that is, her desire to retreat to Hereford. . . . ' I therefore advis'd her, that in case she still was resolv'd, to live as she was : it should be but for a time without imposing on herselfe . . . but 'til then, mind her health, for she began to looke pale and leane.' In other words, having advised her to marry, he appears to cancel the need for such advice by persuading her to stay as she is, rather than decide to go to Hereford.

Now we must ask why the question of marriage suddenly arises ? Why the need for Evelyn's advice ? It is true that during the last few months, Margaret, in her letters, had often dwelt on her ' worldly ' thoughts, and we knew that Godolphin was the cause of them. Furthermore, we felt sure, despite Evelyn's influence, that Godolphin had contrived to meet Margaret on

[1] Elizabeth Evelyn. [2] *Life*, p. 47.

several occasions — the meetings being invariably reflected in her letters. In Margaret's next letter, of 26th
June, we have evidence that Godolphin has ceased to
watch, discern, and soothe, but has taken more definite
action : either he has asked Margaret to allow him to
read all the letters she has written to Evelyn, or perhaps
she suggested that Godolphin should read them to
learn how God was calling her. In any case, she has
asked Evelyn for, and received back her letters : he
still claims them, however : ' I have read over all my
leters and find just caus to wounder why you will keep
them : but here they are for you, only six little short
leters I detain : I will not burn them but doe entreat I may
keep them a little longer : when we meet you shall se
them and giv me leav to dispos of them as I se fit '.
(Evelyn again asked for their return as late as May
1675 but, as we shall learn, by that time she had even
stronger reasons for retaining them). There is trouble
in the air ; this letter of 26th June opens with a sense of
crisis and reveals Margaret's loyalty to Evelyn : ' From
one a cloke till three I was by myselfe upon my knees
before the thron of grace, earnestly interseding for you
and beging pardon for my self '. Evelyn would indeed
be sorrowful, if there were any risk of separation. Her
concern for him implies that Godolphin had made
the offer of marriage, which Margaret rejected in favour
of a retreat to Hereford : ' Your advise I like,' she says
to Evelyn, ' and all you say upon *both subjects*, yet I am
still wher I was, wishing to live alone, I can't but thinke
it most suitable to my humer and the nearest way to
heaven, and you can't blam one so weake as I to chus
that path that will bring me soonest to my Jurneys end,
but be asuerd I will observe your rulls and take your

counsill [1] and will not leav untill *he* giv me free leav to
doe it.' She proceeds in the letter : ' and now I will
tell you what I this day have, if you like it, (not els)
resolved upon : considering how lean I grow and how
litle a tim I have to stay in this part of the world (if I
don't marey) [2] : I will take caer of my looks that the
world may not judg I leav the world unwillingly : if I
doe marey I ought more to take caer of my self that I
may not be disagreeable in his eyes : in order to thes
good looks I speake of — I porpos to sleep 8 hours.'

In the foregoing last four lines, does not Margaret
imply that her present health may be good enough for
Evelyn, but not for Godolphin ? Evelyn omits them,
anyway. Margaret goes on : ' and then drinke red
cows milke : after which it is not good to sleep but
wors to stir, so that my maid shall for an hour read out
of a devine booke to me : then will I rise and till ten be
at my private dutys, then pray with my maids, then by
eleven will I be dresd, then shall I have time before
prayers to read a chapter with diodate [Diodati] [3] and
writ a prayer and colect out of it : and whilst I am
dresing, Becke, [her maid] reads out of the bible and
other good things : at six at night I will for an hour be
at my private dutys, and after that for half an hour or an
hour will learn such things by hart as I would gladly
retain : at nin pray with my peeple, and by myself at

[1] Here we must draw attention to Margaret's ' take your counsill '
altered in the *Life* by Evelyn to ' & so-far your Counsel ', thus protecting
himself against the charge of unduly influencing her. And again, Margaret
says ' will not leav ', but Evelyn writes ' not to determine any-thing
rashly ', implying that her choice was between *marriage* — which he had
advised — and *Hereford*, whereas in fact, she was thinking only of Hereford.

[2] Evelyn omits the last four words.

[3] G. Diodati, *Pious Annotations upon the Holy Bible*. Evelyn presented
this book to her in February 1674, price 12s.

eleven when I come upe : when undresing, as in the
morning, Becke reading to me and then with peace lay
my self down to rest.¹ This for ordinary days, not
fridays, for on that day, and pleys god I will not fail to
fast and pray and on sundays to be early upe, and all the
day well employd, but els on other days this is the rull I
entend to set my self : if as I said before you like it :
and to eat my meat hartely, sens I thanke god I find I can
very well let it alone, and doe wish sensearly I were
setled wher I need use non of thes complacences ; ²
But might atend,³ on god night and day with fasting
and prayer : Before I discovered this in myself, I durs
not giv my self liberty, but sens I thanke god I find not
such plesuers in any of thes injoyments as in tims past
I have don, I hope I may the beter ventuer : for I consider it will not be above three months at the furthest
I shall need to do this (unles it becoms my duty by
being mareyd :) ⁴ and then endeed I shall be always
worldly, but if not, then by the end of the sumer I shall
be at liberty, non will consider my looks nor I shall not
need to caer if they doe, being so far of[f] from them.
let me know what you thinke of all this and let me
quickly hear from you : bid mrs Phesey [Mrs. Veasy,
Evelyn's landlady] cary your leter to Berkeley hous
not saying any thing and they will send it : today I was
zealus I thank god but not tender, I hope it was as well,

¹ Evelyn deletes some stages of this laborious day — performed to his
bidding ; concluding with *Lay me down in peace* ; Margaret's word *rest*
striking him in a vulnerable spot.
² Instead of ' complacences ' Evelyn writes ' impertinencys, the
observances and ceremonys of visits ; formal meales etc. to the expense
of my time ', phrases nowhere in Margaret's letter : so he strengthens her
case against marriage, with which these ' impertinencys ' would interfere.
³ Evelyn writes ' wholy attend '.
⁴ Instead of Margaret's ' unles it becoms my duty by being mareyd ',
Evelyn's credits himself with : ' which is to marry as you would have me '.

for I thanke god I have made good resolutions : dear frind pray god blese you. . . .'

It is not easy for us to guess what Evelyn did think of ' all this '. But it is certain that if the foregoing is a description of how she spent the summer days at Twickenham, Evelyn's influence had lost little of its potency despite Godolphin's offer of marriage.

To revert to the *Life*,[1] Evelyn says that she was now bent upon going to Hereford, ' to which he was wholy averse. . . . I did heartily pitty that worthy Gentleman, and saw no reason in the world, why they should not both be happy in each other, and my Friend composed, without taking any extraordinary or singular course : Tho' on the other hand, when I consider'd thro' what difficultys and reluctancys, this tender creature now in the flower of her beauty, wit and reputation at Court would sacrifice all to God ; I could hardly abstaine from crying out, O *Magnanimous Virgin !* I applaude your designe, I *approve*, I *admire* your choice ' — to give only the beginning of a most rapturous paragraph : it is sufficient to reveal that he preferred a spiritual sequel to his spiritual persuasion.

But what of Evelyn's loneliness when she has gone ? — He laments : ' Why leave you one behind intangl'd in the world ? Whilst you are in the light, I in darkness and a chaös ; for when you are gon ; what is the Court, or the country to your friend ? ' At last he changes his mind : ' Go, go then my holy friend, when you please and be happy '. The irony of it ! His precepts separated her from Godolphin, and now they were to take her from himself. Margaret thus acknowledged her release :

[1] P. 49.

'. . . ten thousand thanks I giv you for your kind
leter, and take your resignation of me to our lord beter
then any thing you can doe for me : for it shows you
the best *christian* and *frind* in the world : they are becoming titles, and almost inseperably worn : I hope god will
endeed refresh you with such comforts as make you
forget all others : how blesed shall we be when we once
com to love nothing but god, thinke of him always :
be ever doeing our duty or wishing for that blesed
employment : it is to be gaind even by flesh and bloud,
let us trye what we can doe : and thou[gh] we fail of
the *elixer*, we shall meet with many raer secrets in this
our devine search, which will aboundantly reward all
the pains we have taken : I beg of god with many tears
that I may love nothing but him, ah that he would hear
me.   He will in tim, he sees and considers me, and when
he thinks fit he will help and deliver me : in the mean-
whill all the days of my apointed tim will I wait till my
change com, even so com oh Lord Jesus, com quickly, oh
let thy kingdom com, and then thy will shall be don by
us on earth as by thy servants in heaven : . . .

' the leters truly I have not had one moment of tim
to read, but when I have I will with speed return them
' god bles you.'

So Evelyn also succumbed to the infectious air of
indecision ; having been ' wholly averse ' to her project, he now says, ' Go when you please '. It is difficult,
if not impossible, to pierce the atmosphere of Twickenham. Godolphin, leaving no word as usual, is typically
inscrutable. In the *Life*, Evelyn is obscure, perhaps
intentionally. He says : ' Thus she continu'd at
Twickenham, (as it were in *probation*) for the most part
retir'd, and somtimes in conversation : *He* [Godolphin]

came often to visite her, and *that* broke her heart ; if he abstain'd from coming, she was still uneasy ; so after some weeks, she returns to London, with full resolutions of beginning her journey.' Now Evelyn, when the moment of parting draws near, cannot bear the thought of losing her. Margaret endeavours to comfort him, with an appeal to put his trust in God :

' I prayd for you presently and did beg of God grace for us all *three* [1] that if he saw it fit, we should as to temporall things, be hapey, and that we might still keep our shaer in his deare Love, why all would bless our gracious god, but if the greatest blessings upon earth would rob us but of one spark of his devine love, I did beseech him for Jesus christ his sake, to strip us even of cloths and let us wander naked through the world : indeed with nothing *but his love* stript of all ornaments but grace, and better were it for us doutles dear frind, how many creatures by custome have had unexpresable misfortunes made tolerable to them, and shall we that profes god and his servis be les able to bear ? no ; I *hop beter things of you*, I question not the brightnes of true piety, and know that peaseobul actions, that is examples perswad men : but let us take heed of trusting to our own vertue in this particular, we must bear with the infirmities of the weake, becom all things to all men, all things are lawfull but not expediant : you dout not I hope that God is able to supply my lack of servis to you, after the darkest night the sun shins forth : and *there is no remembrance of pain when the child is born*, in heaven you know we shall be *crowned*, and we shall never part : when we are weak god is strong : he raised you up a frind of nothing, and he can comfort you without that

[1] Evelyn, Godolphin, and Margaret.

frind : if times are bad we must [be] contented to bear
our part : you did ill to mention long suffering in your
text : for that is now our bisnes, *charity suffereth long and
is kind*, see what follows, seeketh not her own, do you
beleev I shall not be broken at parting : *what do you take
me for* ? but God is the healer of our deadly wounds . . .
asuer your selfe I shall weep perpetualy when I think
of you [qualifying with] that is, for the most part
and will pray for you night & day, and will labour to
inspire my betty [1] with all the love and duty imaginable
to you, and when I am dead she shall be a *testimony* how
well I thought of my frind, that is in case of this cruel
separation I speak of, but who knows it may be god has
better things in store for us, that is pleasanter ones : . . .

Yet again Evelyn seems to change his mind. On
further reflection that there would be no more happy
hours at Berkeley House, he felt he could not, after all,
be parted from her. ' It grives me ', writes Margaret,
' to se you upon reflection chang your mind, for you
told me you would not but consent to what I said, and
now you take all that we said to another light, and like
non of those reasons which before you seemed to aprove
of. I have no better to give, but if you will I am content
to repeal them.'

But there was no need. Lady Berkeley, the observant
concierge, from her vantage points at Berkeley House
and Twickenham Park, saw more of the game than the
participants. As a thrice-married woman she probably
harboured little sympathy for Evelyn's friendship, even
if she did not view it with positive distaste. If Margaret,
at moments, under Evelyn's influence was fanatically
celibate, the experienced Lady Berkeley saw in her the

[1] Elizabeth, Evelyn's daughter.

potential wife. And so did Godolphin ; as a man of the world, he would not have wasted his time in wooing a pathological case. In her heart, and perhaps in silence, Lady Berkeley commiserated with Margaret. With Godolphin she would not be unsympathetic, though impatient at his unending patience. However, she was thankful that, whether by contrivance or accident, he had avoided foreign service during these critical months. But why did he allow Evelyn to continue to sway Margaret from one mood to another ? Lady Berkeley decided that the nearer Margaret remained to Godolphin the better. Therefore she appealed to her not to desert Berkeley House ; besides, she loved her. The impressionable girl capitulated :

' Sens I writ thus far many new things have hapned : I was cald to supper and after supper my Lady Berkeley askt me questions, and told me that without failing if I did think of leaving her for above a month, she would never endure me, that she never did think of my going hardly without tears, and that she loved me as her heart, and how could I resolve to leav her, and why would I be so mad to go by myself, I shold not go — I know she speaks true, she is perfectly true, she would not lye for ten such houses as she has :

' Now I think sens god has been pleysd to aford me such a frind and many opportunities of *seeing my best frind*,[1] I shall not do wisly to run into a chang unles for *a best frind*,[2] which cant be yet of many years I fear . . . she told me she was overjoyd, and begd me to never think again of leaving her, for she could not enduer it, upon her word she loved me dearly : I began to consider that this was all I could wish from a christian, that

---

[1] Evelyn.   [2] Godolphin.

I was very young to live all alone : without ever seeing
my best frind that I had implored god almightys consell —
that I hopt I took the middle way, if at least I stayd for
some time longer : but to my sister [1] I do sertainly go
for a month :

' Now to all this you must speak & tell me what you
think and whether I do well or ill, and be sure no letter
coms from you *without a world of kindness,* the last was a
prodigy of love, but I fear my friend (from my very
heart I speak it) what you said to our dear god was a
litle too full — I want a word — 'twas too passionat, I
was sorry it was so, the afliction was not sertain, and we
did but talk, and endeed I fear you were too rash to tell
all that to god — and now I have said this take it as
the greatest mark of my love that I can give you . . .

' Now for tusday I am still what I was, say you what
you will, hours and days moov dully on . . .'

[1] No indication as to which, and not mentioned in the *Life*, p. 52 :
perhaps Henrietta Maria Blagge, Lady Yarborough.

CHAPTER VII

THE OMINOUS CALM
1674-75

MARGARET not only appeased Lady Berkeley by deciding not to go to Hereford ; she delighted Evelyn, who knew that, despite the strains and stresses of the last few weeks, he had gained a moral victory. Margaret's attachment to him seemed stronger than ever. When her choice lay between Godolphin and Hereford, she chose Hereford ; when Evelyn advised her to stay, she obeyed him : and even when he had agreed to let her go it was as much due to her consideration for him as for Lady Berkeley that she dropped the project altogether.

But we must credit Lady Berkeley with common sense and plain-speaking — qualities that had the greater effect upon Margaret, who experienced little of either from Evelyn. If Evelyn was delighted with the prospect of a renewal of his weekly visits, Lady Berkeley was perfectly satisfied in playing for a long-term result, secretly hoping that, sooner or later, Godolphin would bring these visits to an end.

Margaret's ' I shall not do wisely to run into a chang unles for a best frind which cant be yet of many years I fear ', at least gave Lady Berkeley hope that marriage was still possible, even if it were far distant. For the marriage, once Margaret broke away from Evelyn and became amenable, was contingent on Godolphin's purchase of the office of Master of the Robes, which could not be reasonably expected for a year or so. In the meantime, however, Margaret would have, as she declared, 'many opportunities of seeing my best frind'.

Evelyn lost no time in attempting to reassert his influence. He suggested that when her Twickenham holiday was over, Margaret should stay at Sayes Court, 'not being able (as she affirmed)', he says, 'to comply any longer with the receiving, & returning formal & impertinent visits, and other avocations, which took-up all her time at London ; tho' with a Lady who so much esteemed and cherish'd her'.[1] Lady Berkeley was not to be so easily outwitted, and at once opposed his suggestion. Evelyn says she 'could not suffer this eclipse, or endure' that Margaret 'should go from her with any patience'. Lady Berkeley, in her wisdom, obviously deemed the Deptford country air unsuitable for Margaret at this juncture ! Some idea of the problem with which Lady Berkeley had to deal, and which she hoped to solve, may be gathered from Margaret's outburst when Lady Berkeley rejected Evelyn's offer of accommodation : 'My *best friend*, as to my being in your family, it was *almost*, and *ah !* that it had not ben *almost*, but *altogether !* '[2]

It is only to be expected that the *Diary* throws no light upon the summer crisis of 1674 ; indeed our exasperation at Evelyn's obscurity is only intensified by an enigmatic entry of 16th July : 'To *Lond* : sent for by Margaret, return'd that evening, not well pleas'd, upon an unjust report', which may well be relevant, but defies interpretation.

[1] *Life*, p. 51.   [2] *Life*, p. 52.

H

Meanwhile, Lady Berkeley did not allow Margaret
in her present low state of health to see too much of
Evelyn, or let the solitude of Twickenham Park overwhelm her. They were together at Southborough by
9th August to drink the Waters — though admittedly
it was a doubtful benefit for one so ascetically pale
and lean as Margaret.

Evelyn, temporarily denied his usual pilgrimage to
Berkeley House, and perhaps at a loose end, took the
opportunity to visit some of his friends and property
in Kent and Sussex. Between 6th–8th August he journeyed to Groombridge, Tunbridge Wells (he did not
drink the Waters), and Lewes. Coming north and
homeward, on the 9th, it was not at all by chance that
he happened to be near Southborough ; of course, he
paid Margaret a visit, for he had not seen her since 16th
July. A few days later Evelyn was among the thousand
spectators at Windsor, watching, with great excitement,
the mock battle of the storming of Maestricht (just
fallen to the French) specially staged below the Castle,
with all realism. Pepys was present, too, and afterwards
returned to London with Evelyn.

Apart from an occasional meeting, or a business
letter to Pepys (as Secretary to the Navy) concerning
the sick and wounded prisoners, Evelyn, at this period,
was not yet an intimate friend of his : but their friendship was to grow with the years. Although they shared
antiquarian interests, in temperament and character they
were poles apart : their friendship was formed on the
attraction of opposites. (Of course, by 1674 we must
allow for a natural cooling of Samuel Pepys' blood.)
Evelyn would call Nell Gwynn ' an impudent come-
dian ' ; Pepys would say ' she looked pretty in her

shift'. Thus Pepys is praised for his defects, Evelyn is censured for his virtues. Pepys laid bare his soul in one revelation. Evelyn was more subtle ; he makes us dig for his. Evelyn admired in Pepys his free, open manner and his lively inquisitiveness. ' O fortunate Mr. Pepys,' he says, ' who knows, possesses and enjoys all that's worth seeking after ; let me live among your inclinations, I shall be happy.' Pepys, with no capacity to scale the heights of ' ΑΓΑΠΑ ', could yet admire Evelyn, and say : ' He is so much above others, he must be allowed a little for a little conceited-ness'. One was plagued by a passion, the other enjoyed it.

Margaret now pledged her loyalty to Evelyn : ' For you . . . there is nothing that I know of I would not do. I would denigh myself any pleasure without exeption for you, and undergo all I am capable of enduring . . . for to my death I will love you.' Yet, as she continues, we feel that Godolphin still retains her heart : she says she is Evelyn's friend, ' the best title I can have next that of a Christian, and for all I have I would not lose you '.[1]

Although Margaret spent the remainder of August at Twickenham in the Godolphin circle with Lady Berkeley and Lady Fitzhardinge (the wife of Godolphin's cousin the third Viscount Fitzhardinge) and at Moor Park with the Duchess of Monmouth, apparently she derived little benefit or relaxation : from Twickenham on 1st September she wrote to Evelyn :

' . . . I am mightely disturbed in my mind by thes perpeatull hureys that I am in, never at rest nor peace, but I hope one day to be quiat : I am now in great afliction

[1] Letter to Evelyn, 12th August 1674.

for mr godolphin's prity sister [1] whom he lovs of all things, is sicke of a malignant feaver they fear she will dye, the chief design of this leter is to beg your prayers for her, if she dys he will be poor man in great afliction and is now in great aprehension : I have bin today so sorey with him, and for him, that I can scarce se . . .' On which we may comment : pity is akin to love.

By 9th September Margaret had returned from Twickenham to Berkeley House ; on that day she wrote to Evelyn :

'. . . I reseive[d] both your leters. . . . I thanke you mightely, your prayers are heard, the yong prity sister is alive and in a very fair way of recovery : I am in town and am com for all together, I shall be very hartely glad to se you on friday or saterday about six or seven a cloke, for then I shall be in my chamber of cours ; and we may with out any inconveanance pray together if you se fit : this in case you are in town at that tim : if not why then I shall expect you on tusday as I usd to doe, only I could wish you would com at six a cloke derectly upe to my chamber and not dine here, but com then so we might pray together, for I would willingly have our first meeting consecrated with prayers and thanksgivings : forgiv my hast, diner stays, let me hear what you will doe.'

Thus Margaret took care that Lady Berkeley's dis-approval should not interfere with Evelyn's 'first meeting' at Berkeley House since 16th July ; instead of dining at noon with the Berkeleys and Margaret, Evelyn was invited to an evening of candlelight and prayer : on Tuesday, 15th September, the two long months of separation came to an end.

[1] Probably Penelope Godolphin (d. 1697).

In the previous May Evelyn's *Navigation and Commerce* — an introduction to a history of the Dutch War begun at the King's bidding (and not to be refused) as long ago as 1670 — had been published, and he could now turn to something nearer to his heart. He began to plan a new series of meditations for Margaret. They would be similar in form to his earlier efforts, but of greater length and interest. He would tell her the story of the seven days of Creation, each part describing one day's creation. The second [1] day's creation formed Monday's meditation, the third day's creation that for Tuesday, and so on. Between September 1674 and July 1675 he completed the story of four days' creation : in due course we will look into it.

With Margaret re-established in Berkeley House in early September Evelyn adopted the routine of spending four or five days alternately in London and Deptford, maintaining his monthly average of four or five visits to her apartment.

On 16th October, the second year of their friendship was duly recorded in the *Diary* : ' Anniversarie M. inviol ' : inviolable, his favourite word, meaning, to be kept sacred from profanation. How far had he succeeded ? Margaret's anniversary letter hardly confirmed his success :

' I giv my frind a thousand thanks for his kind leter and for the present [2] in it : which I hope I shall not be so unfortunat as to loos : . . . As to improvments, for if not, why doe you put me upon the repetition of what I have so often acknowledgd to you : I know you will

---

[1] Only the 2nd-5th days survive.
[2] Perhaps the engraved sardonyx, recorded in the *Diary* on 31st October 1674.

say 'tis not I but god, tis true frind, it is god and to him be the glory of it, but doe we always remember that when we our selfs are comended, *forgiv me this wrong* but you desierd to be told of your faults, and for ought I know this is non of them, but judging you by my self, I fear that somtims ther may be self love in thos things wherin we imagin we only intend gods glory, but least I insuer you by judging thus hardly of you . . .'

Now there is another glaring instance of Evelyn's use of Margaret's words out of their context and for his own purpose. Two months after this letter was written, she took part at Court in Crowne's pastoral *Calisto*, an undertaking for her which Evelyn describes as a 'vanity', and to which he says she was averse (as we shall read more fully presently). In the *Life*,[1] to emphasize her antipathy to acting, he uses the following passage from this letter of 16th October : 'I blese god I grow daily les fond of the world, more thankfull to god, les caerfull for outward things and more thirsty after the blesed sacrament, not as I was wont becaus I had many sins to be pardond, nor becaus I held it my duty, but out of a desire to cõmemorat my saviours death, and to be again entertained with the wounderfull plesuers that I feel ther and no wher els : all worldly joys, all splendid ornaments, titles, and honours would I bring to the feet of my crusifyd saviour.'

Margaret continues : 'besids I am not so formall in my devotions, so scrupleous, and so soon discomposd as I was wont to be : and I am in my opinion les *weary of the world* and my life then I was, and yet more *willing to leav all* and be with christ, which is best of all : all thes

I thinke I owe to your prayers and medetations, advice, and example . . . for the prayers of som frinds I have, I doe infinitly esteem and hold them to be great use to me : but chiefely to you my best frind that ever yet I had, I owe to you : and now I hope you have by this tim suffi[ci]ent caus of joy and will I know most harteley prais god for this his mersey to you :

'But ah let not your devotions wholy consist of praises, but offer upe many petitions for me also, who am yet cold and wandering in my prayers, peevch [peevish] to my servants, vain in my thoughts, backward to holy dutys, apt to relaps and grow worldly : fond of som things to a madnes, consernd very often for the trifles of this life and soon discomposd, the tim would fail to confes all my imperfections : against which I beg you will pray our lord to defend me that prais him for you, and asuer you I am and always will be yours in christ : forgiv my blots I had no light.'

So her usual gratitude to Evelyn is expressed, though she cannot refrain from gently criticizing his innate pride in the efforts on her behalf. But there is a renewed note of resignation, almost of desperation, in her willingness ' to leave all '. She is in a mood when unalloyed friendship is felt to be imperfect, unsatisfying. Perhaps she is still thinking of Godolphin, who continued to avoid foreign service during these critical months ; and even if a visit to Margaret might not yet meet with its former welcome, it is quite likely that, occasionally, he wrote to her. Unable to set up house on his present salary as Groom of the Bedchamber, he had set his heart on the office of Master of the Robes, and any hint or chance of success would provide the subject of an

enticing letter, or indeed the basis of a tangible offer.
When Margaret tells Evelyn of her disposition 'to
grow worldly', there is, as usual, only one interpretation, that she is again thinking of marriage and
Godolphin.

Evelyn had no confidence that he could retain Margaret's affections for ever. From its inception the
friendship had caused him anxiety. Even with Godolphin out of the way, her moods alternated between
rapture and self-deprecation. The friendship made no
real and tranquil progress. The effects of a holiday at
Twickenham were not easily effaced. Too often had he
to use the confessional whip. And if he lacerated her
feelings, he could never permanently reform them.
Constituted as he was, he had no conception of the effect
of his constant preaching : that the young rebel in the
end. Yet he continued to use the whip. The summer
crisis of 1674 — when he almost lost her — called for a
greater crack than ever :

'But above all, the sins I have committed since I
have tasted of thy love : in those I knew I had offended,
but in these who it is I sinned against, even one, who by
his many mercys has prevented my ruine, & drawne
me from death forceably, yet gently, and with the cords
of love ; one that has called after me, & when I have
turn'd a little has not shown his angry, but inviting face,
& sweetly compell'd me by aboundant kindnesse. . . .
Lord, I will sin no more, I will be Thine ; make me
but partaken of Thyselfe, and I shall never abandon
thee againe. . . .' [1]

What effect this chastisement had upon her, we do

[1] *An Eucharisticall Office*, p. 215 ; an addition probably made in the
autumn of 1674.

not know. Certainly Evelyn would display no great
sensitiveness for her feelings. Whatever she thought of
the hopelessness of reconciling his spiritual spurs with
the advice in his letters, she did not commit herself in
writing ; or, if she did so, Evelyn destroyed the letter.
It is a noteworthy fact that the surviving letters which
can be assigned to this period are very few. This
scarcity, continued as it was for several months, may be
of some significance. Apart from her inclination to
' worldliness ' the friendship seemed to be going on
much as usual. Margaret's health had certainly improved and in consequence, she again exhibited a
distaste or incapacity for spiritual delights. Nevertheless, Evelyn's weekly Berkeley House visits, his dining
or supping with Margaret, and their reading and
praying together, relieved the autumn afternoons and
evenings with accustomed regularity ; Evelyn wrote
his offices and Meditations with greater industry than
ever.

In November he sent his first instalment on the
Creation to Margaret.

Her acknowledgment was sent in due course :

' The medetation you sent me is I thinke without a
fault, and then you may believ I am without words, for
when I cant doe a thing well I let it quite alone if I can
that is : by which rull I shold not awnser your leter for
tis imposiable to doe it well :

' I never *was so reproacht* in all my life and could I
thinke myself guilty of a fault to my frind there is non
upon earth would be more willing to acknowledg it
then I, but truly I can not *thinke my self guilty* in any of
the perticulars you seem so *biterly* to accuse me of, but
how ever we will talke of thes things for I dont afect

writing upon such ocations : *the leter I will keep* if you pleys *but I desire you may not* : . . .

'Your articles and leter we will discours upon : on friday I was sory for my sins but for my life could not be soft, doe what I could, I read thought prayd did all that lay in my power but did not obtain thos blesings I desiered, but yet I hope I was acepted : on saterday I usd your rogation ofice and the prayer for publicke humileations you made and I thanke god said them hartely : on sonday I reseived the blesesd sacrament at linconsine [Lincoln's Inn]: at the holy table I recomended you and yours most earnestly to almighty god, and dont dout but you were at the sam *time upon your knees at your mental* comunion :

'I have no more to say at this time but that I am as much your frind as ever I was, and I ever will be so, if you continu good and I lover of goodness : which without gods grace we can neither of us doe and there-fore god of his infinet mersey grant it us for the sake of his dear son Jesus Christ our lord amen.'

Again Margaret has committed some misdemeanour — in Evelyn's eyes — and of which he has accused her bitterly. In herself, she is hardening ; her devotions are still of little benefit to her. The naïveté of her ' I am as much your frind as ever I was and ever will be so if you continu good and I lover of goodnes ' must not mislead us ; in her artless way, it is a criticism of Evelyn's present conduct — not unconnected, perhaps, with his ' bitter ' accusation ; and that she may have real doubts of reconciling her love for Godolphin with her ability to sustain Evelyn's ideal of goodness.

There is further evidence, in another letter of the autumn of 1674, of her spiritual apathy. Her health is

obviously improved, and, in consequence, her continued attempted flights of piety are either irksome
or inadequate.

'You [1] might well believ you were more then
ordinarley asisted when you writ the prayer you spoke
of, for endeed it is mighty good and so soon as ever I
have don my leter I entend to use it, for god knows I
need it mighteley having now upon me a *dismall sadnes* :
I know not what to doe I have it so often. I thanke god
'tis not from any great sin I comit, becaus (though I
often *fall*) yet I persist in no sin and I know in that case
god is mercifull : but I believ it is my constitution :
this I know that what ever the caus of my *diseas* is,
prayer is my remedey : and as you have said god never
suffers his servants to go away sad :

'The other prayer you sent is a very good one, I will
giv them both to maney that I know pray god blese you
for them :

'The lord help me I am *seldom ever satisfyd* with my
self : for I ever am in my opinion too *merey* or *too sad* :
the world I valu not, som fuw frinds I love intierly, for all
other things methinks I am indiferent : they love me
again I am perswayded, why then am I sad ? god knows,
I am suer I doe not : but this I know that in this earthly
tabernacle I shall always grone till I am *clothd* upon with
my hous which is from heaven : and yet not to mak

[1] This is the only surviving letter bearing Margaret's seal — which was
a present from Evelyn on 27th January 1674 : it cost 10s. For notes on
the motto and words of the seal — which are the same as those used to
accompany the pentacle, see *Life*, pp. 214-15.

myself beter then I am, 'tis not so eager a thirst after things devine as a *wearynes* of all things I se here : wether that proceed from my loving only god or no I daer not determin, but I *fear* it dos not : for it is not all days alike :

'Dear mr Evelyn you will have litle reason to like my leters, I fear, for of late they are rather complaints then frindly leters : but liberty you have given me you know, and I take it you se : god in heaven blese you I am going to prayers for us both.'

It is conceivable that in the autumn of 1674, as Lady Berkeley noticed the improvement in Margaret's health and the colour returning to her cheeks, she arranged for the *Mary Beale* portrait, to which we have already referred, to be painted. At all costs, Lady Berkeley decided to improve on Dixon's portrait — with its emphasis on death and funeral urn : that was the way Evelyn ' dressed ' it (or allowed Margaret to do so). Lady Berkeley would have something more attractive ; a challenge to Evelyn let it be : the portrait of a potential wife. And, there it is, in silks and curls — signs of Margaret's ' worldliness ', indeed of revolt. And best of all, a Cupid ! Was that the Godolphin touch ? Evelyn must have turned away in disgust. Some time later, Godolphin again indulged this delicate sense of humour by presenting Evelyn with a painting, by Guido Reni, of a Cupid sleeping !

The scarcity of letters of any importance from Margaret persisted into the latter part of the year. In the previous summer she judiciously retained six of her letters retrieved from Evelyn. Perhaps she has been taught a lesson ; in November she confessed to Evelyn that she does not ' afect ' writing upon all ' ocations '.

Furthermore, she forbade Evelyn to keep a copy of the letter in which he had reproached her. And it is remarkable that, unlike the letters covering the earlier stages of the friendship, there is practically nothing of interest in the later ones which is not given in the *Life*.

Margaret now began to rehearse the part of Diana, Goddess of Chastity, in John Crowne's *Calisto*, a pastoral comedy to be performed at Court before their Majesties. According to Evelyn in the *Life*, ' it was not possible to leave her out, who had upon the like solemnity formerly (and when maid of honor) acquitted herselfe, with so universal applause and admiration '. However, this invitation to resume contact with the place ' she had now intirely taken leave of ', continues Evelyn, ' put a mortification upon her . . . but there was no refusing '. The King and the Duke of Monmouth commanded her to appear as *Diana*, the other players being ' of the most illustrious quality '. The cast of eighteen included the princesses Mary and Anne (daughters of the Duke of York), Sarah Jennings (afterwards Duchess of Marlborough), the Countess of Derby, and the Duke of Monmouth. The gentlemen were rehearsed by the famous actor Betterton, the princesses and ladies by his wife. Mrs. Evelyn, in her own manner, told her friend Bohun of the noble company, ' among which Mistress Blagge's severity is constrained to make one '.[1] Mrs. Evelyn, good critic that she was, added that ' the dances, scenes, musick, singing are extraordinary and in their kind excel the poet's industrie or genius '.

Doubtless Margaret brought an appealing sincerity to her part ; Evelyn says ' never was there anything more charming and divertisant than to heare her at any

[1] 24th February 1675.

time recite or reade a dramatiq poem'; memory, judgment, accent, motion, sweetness, and grace — all were hers. In the play she wore a magnificent costume of gold and silver lace and brocade, adorned with *point d'Espagne*, £20,000 worth of jewels, and a plume of scarlet and white; she carried a bow, and a quiver of sixteen arrows. There is little doubt that Mary Beale's portrait of her must have been overshadowed.

Evelyn (now settled in his new lodging in Bell Yard, King Street, Westminster) saw two performances in December — probably dress rehearsals — to which the Court were invited. The *prima donna* temperament of the amateur actresses caused a certain amount of delay: Margaret says the 'alterations are many; the ladys not disposd to act som of them'. The official 'first-night' probably took place at Shrovetide, 1675; and there were repetitions, with new costumes, as late as in the following April. Margaret was greatly perturbed at losing, during one of the dress rehearsals, a diamond worth £80 belonging to the Countess of Suffolk. But all was well when the Duke of Monmouth made it good by sending its value to the Countess.

It is indeed sad to reflect that, if we believe Evelyn's habitual word,[1] Margaret found no great joy in her acting. 'So soon as ever she could get cleare of the stage, without complementing any creature, or trifling with the rest, who stay'd the collation and refreshments that were prepared: away she slips like a spirit to Berkeley House, and to her Oratory; whither I waited on her, and left her on her knees, thanking God, that she was delivered from this vanity, and with her B.

[1] *Life*, p. 55.

Saviour againe : Never (says she) will I come into this
tempation more, whilst I breathe.'

There is some inconsistency here ; Evelyn had
overlooked that on 11th December, when *Calisto* was
fully rehearsed, four days before he himself (wearing
a new pair of the best woven silk stockings and buckles) [1]
first witnessed it, thought it necessary to make his own
commentary on such worldly diversion, presenting it
to Margaret in the *Meditation upon the Advents* :
'. . . how different indeede are the visites of the
Lord, and of his Spirit, from the visites of the World,
full of vanity and trifling emptinesse, and sinn : Teach
me, o Lord, as never to grieve, much lesse to reject those
sweete communications of Thy Grace ; so to avoyd as
much as in me lies, complacences in any creature,
adherance to any object, when they stand in competition
with my duty to Thee. . . .' Another passage in the
same work reveals that the rigour of Evelyn's spiritual
advice to a young and delicate girl could cut as sharply
as his whip : ' Heaven only is the happy state, and pity
and virtue the way to it ; whatever be the obstacle,
remove it ; whatever ye difficulty, despise it ; strive
for ye mastery, there is a crown of glory at the end of
ye race, be temperate, chast, grow leane, suffer hunger,
thirst, poverty, scorne losse of all, nay of thy very life
if it stand in competition '. If we prefer to set aside
Evelyn's word, her distaste for acting and collations
derived from her ignominious position in having left
the Court two years previously to reappear there as
still unmarried. According to the *Life*,[2] rumours were
flying that she and Godolphin were already married.

Before leaving Crowne's *Calisto*, we must draw

attention to some of the author's unconsciously comic
lines, which, perhaps, fell upon Godolphin's receptive
ear :

> Kind lovers, love on,
> Lest the world be undone,
> And mankind be lost by degrees :
> For if all from their loves
> Should go wander in groves,
> There soon would be nothing but trees.

In the *Meditation for Wednesday*, Evelyn describes the
splendour of the heavens in his new, impressive style,
though again he cannot forbear to show himself tortured at the imperfections of Margaret and the possibility that the world may yet claim her. These words
are for reading aloud at Berkeley House : ' . . . God
is Love : Ah ! Thou fairest of Men, Thou whom my
Soule loveth : when shall I come to behold, and enjoy
this Light, this Love, this Beauty, all these perfections,
and no more admire these low objects, the sensual and
inferiour satisfactions of this world, falsely so called,
which is vanity, which is nothing : Take, O take off
my heart and turne away my eyes, my affections, and
inclynations from these transitory things, and fix them
upon thee, who onely are lovely, and perfection in the
abstract, and alone canst fill all our capacities '.
Evelyn must have thought there was no stability in
human nature. Not only was he still concerned to keep
Margaret's eyes from worldly objects and her thoughts
from worldly desires ; the insecurity of her affection
for himself continued to plague him. What benefit,
serenity, or pleasure could he derive from the friendship
when he felt bound to goad her unceasingly into
obedience with such words as these ? ' The person

and interest of my onely friend (who is as my owne Soule) let me looke upon *as my soule*, and to whom nothing is more due than my fidelity, never let me faile to continue it by my prayers, my counsel, my avowed esteeme, and all other offices of sincerity, and the most Christian endearments : so few are there whose friendships are combin'd in Thee, that 'tis no wonder to find that most blessed of relations on earth, so often violated and betrayed : preserve therefore to me my deare friend. . . .' Evelyn was a virtuoso in everything except psychology.

In the new year of 1675 the lack of letters from Margaret becomes still more marked, and puzzling : we are completely in the dark. We feel bound to ask : What is happening ? There is not a word of Godolphin, though it cannot be doubted that he continued to keep a sharp watch upon the two friends in an inconspicuous manner. Of course, a note from Lady Berkeley would tell him all he wanted to know. Evelyn's visits to Berkeley House go on as usual — or nearly as usual. Instead of dining with Margaret at midday, spending the afternoon with her, and returning to Deptford in the early evening, between 26th February and the spring days of March, he indulged five times in the unusual practice of having supper with her. On such evenings he avoided the dismal prospect of the return journey home to Deptford, by staying with her until it was time to retrace his steps down St. James', over the Mall, and across St. James' Park to his lodgings in King Street, Westminster, for the night. These spring supper parties ceased on 31st March, and for some reason he did not sup with her again until 1st June — and a great deal had happened by then, as we shall see. Even if the risk of

I

Margaret's ' cheap ' thoughts no longer existed, Godolphin, on hearing of this series of *soupers à deux* at
Berkeley House on a spring evening, could hardly
remain unperturbed. But if he were perturbed, he
would never let anyone see it. He would exhibit
' great prudence and dexterity, without noise '.[1] Un-
ruffled, as at cards or at Newmarket, he would determine
if Margaret were really happy. He would never allow
her conflicts and indecisions to disturb his equanimity.
When she imagined herself happy with Evelyn, we may
assume that Godolphin maintained his habitual detachment. When she tired of Evelyn's preaching, Godolphin almost certainly would make things easy for her
by a greater approachability : he would be eminently
accessible. It is indeed not unlikely that he would practically manœuvre her into asking him to marry her :
it was Godolphin's way. In his later years, ' he invariably declined with almost invincible obstinacy every
post which was sure to be forced on him '.[2]

[1] Letter : Evelyn to Godolphin, 16th June 1696.
[2] W. S. Churchill, *Life of Marlborough*, vol. ii, p. 74.

CHAPTER VIII

MARRIAGE

1675

WE cannot do more than conjecture that Godolphin knew of the springtime suppers. Furthermore, we can only guess what sin Margaret committed and mentioned to Evelyn in her letter of 13th March 1675 :

' This day I always com upe (if nothing of exstrodinary hinders me) at 5 a cloke : to bewail the sins of my wholl life and to thinke of death, and by that medetation to fit my self for the *rest* of sunday, it being the reserection day of our lord : when looking upon som devine leters of yours I met with one of the 10 of Feb. in which there was much goodnes : it made me weep very tenderly, it made me ashamed : for in it ther is great comendations of my piety and goodnes : but when I reflected not only upon my sins many years past, but thos which I daily fall into, I had no rest in my spiret till I had resolvd to undeseiv you, and to let you know how wicked I am, how worthy of your pity, how unworthy of your comendation : I have this week comited a fault which thes two years I have not don, I know it was a fault and yet I did it : now what is to be thought of one so wicked as I am, who will wilfully sin against gods grace : I am in great afliction and doe hate myself for this thing, and yet I hope god will pardon it, for I have shed many tears, and am ful of the sens of my saviours merits, truly humble and ther is nothing I doe abhor like comendation : I could not help leting you know this, first for your prayers, but chiefly that you might no longer set a valu and esteem upon me, for I am not fit to live upon the earth : speake not to me of *this*, when you se me, for I shall be so much aflicted that I shall not be fit to go down to super, but pray for me if perhaps I may be pardond: I am astonishd I am alive.' ...

Margaret certainly refers to the occasion two years before, in March 1673, when we assumed that she eluded Evelyn and met Godolphin — an assumption fairly confirmed by her own confession to ' a week of foly and madnes ' : on her return, it will be remembered, she made use of Evelyn's penitential Office. May we not assume that, for the second springtime, Margaret's fancy lightly turned to thoughts of Godolphin ? Perhaps the ' fault ' was nothing less than the humanizing physic of a secular kiss : and the kiss was Godolphin's. But it is significant that she is more embarrassed than penitent this time. Formerly, a kiss from Godolphin would make her exclaim : ' The first moment I am tried, I am forgetful of the Creator '. Now her request to Evelyn before going down to supper with the Berkeleys : ' Speak not to me of this . . . for I shall be so much aflicted ' signifies a reluctance to discuss, rather than true penitence : the least said the soonest mended.

Again we can only guess the probable course of events between March and May 1675. As Evelyn's visits to Berkeley House are reduced to two in April, perhaps Margaret, discovering a latent liking for the physic which she had not taken for at least two years, saw Godolphin again. In two months' time — in June — he was to leave England on a mission to The Hague : any hint of his departure would undoubtedly be conveyed to Margaret. With the crack of Evelyn's whip still in her ears, she might well begin to look upon Godolphin as a haven. His projected journey, his calm, comforting personality, would intensify her desire for shelter. His silence is exasperating. Did he diagnose her struggle of the body against the spirit, and tell her, gently, that neither must win ; that if one was victorious, the triumph was sterile ?

Whatever the predisposing causes, suppers, spring-time fancy, spiritual whip, humanizing physic, or Godolphin's impending foreign service, Margaret and he were married on 16th May 1675. The ceremony, conducted by Dr. Lake (one of the Duke's chaplains) at the Temple Church, was witnessed only by Lady Berkeley and Margaret's maid, Beck. Evelyn was not informed ; in fact, the marriage was a secret which remained inviolate for nearly twelve months.

No victory at cards or at Newmarket could have given Godolphin greater satisfaction. He was un-doubtedly a man of perception, who could diagnose all artifice, motive, and ingratiation. He was credited with great skill in finding out what were the King's inclinations — which he was very ready to comply with ; the same skill worked now. Once the drift of the friendship was discovered, Margaret was whisked into safety from under Evelyn's nose. The couple, however, went on exactly as before. Godolphin kept out of the way, and Margaret allowed Evelyn to visit her as usual at Berkeley House. But there was this difference : the newly married couple and Lady Berke-ley now constituted an audience by whom a secret is shared. Even the simple Beck's heart must have fluttered every time she showed Evelyn into Margaret's apartments. They could watch, perhaps with suppressed glee, the reactions of Evelyn, a protagonist in ignorance of the secret. Glee or pity ? pity for his blindness : or did he deserve to be kept in ignorance ?

It is well-nigh incredible that Margaret should keep Evelyn in ignorance, but that she could do so implies that she married of her own will. If Godolphin had pressed her to marry, there would have been little need for secrecy ; indeed, in that case she would have needed Evelyn's solace. The break, therefore, was practically a revolt, something she could not yet bring herself to confess ; something that only time alone could soften. She had broken the pact too : had she not declared to Evelyn at the Altar of Friendship that, in the event of her marriage, ' you shall be witness ' ? What struggle prefaced this violation ? What had this sensitive creature sacrificed ? We may believe there was no sacrifice : had she not often fallen from grace since October 1672 ? Evelyn's delineation of her saint-like character in the *Life* may now seem too generous ; it is certainly at variance with her spiritual failings as reflected in her letters and his Offices and Meditations. Perhaps the rightness of her cause both justified the violation of the pact and prevented confession. At any rate, to continue to meet Evelyn as though nothing had happened, her powers of acting would be highly necessary.

They were soon called upon. Two days after the marriage, with wonderful self-assurance, she invited Evelyn and his wife, ranting Nanny Howard, the feckless Lady Yarborough (Margaret's elder sister) and others to a collation — as Evelyn records in the *Diary*. And two days later, the Evelyns entertained Margaret, Lady Berkeley, Lady Yarborough, and Nan Howard at

Sayes Court. Godolphin, preparing for his journey to
The Hague, astutely kept out of the way.

A fortnight after the marriage, Evelyn suddenly
thought of his collection of Margaret's six letters
retained by her and still in her keeping, and asked her
to return them. Her reply is sufficiently tenacious to
imply that Evelyn did not get them :

' I doe acknowledg you have by your perpetuatul
pains in writing and studying good medetations, prayers,
leters, and all thos holy offices of love for my souls good
for ever oblidgd me, and I were the worst of wemen if I
shold refuse to *lay down my life for you*, who have so
largly contributed thrugh the merits of christ Jesus to
the saving of my soul : and when I have said this you
may be sertain thos papers you desier are at your servis
if you pleys ; but why shold you desier them ? doe I
not writ often to you ? can you not take out what ever
you like of them with out putting any marke upon them
whose they were ? I have som undenighable reasons
why I would willingly have them, and sens my carecter
you have, and what ever is said in thos papers you may
take out if you pleys, why shold you continu obstinat :
I must undoutdly giv them you if you still persist : but
why will you be so resolutly set upon a thing which I
have begd you will be pleysd to be with out : I dont
know that ever I writ any leter to you in my life, that
did not asuer you of my prayers for you : and in which
I did not acknowledg how much I had bin beholding to
you upon religious acounts : why then must just thos
papers be torn from me ? : all that I can say is, they are at
your servis if you pleys to have them, but remember an
English proverb of much adoe about nothing, and se if
your case is not like it, pray let me perswayd you out of

this idle fansey : you know who [1] writs to me somtims :
I asuer you I have burnt every one of his leters but two
or three that are in a maner prayers, and which (when I
have time) I will writ out, and then burn the origanls, [2]
and suer I am you dont dout of my kindnes to him,
though maybe you will now . . . : consider of this,
and remember I am tyd to be your frind upon god
almightys acount and therfore as long as you are his
servant, I must be your frind.'

If we look into this matter of Margaret's letters as
given in the *Life*, [3] we shall see that Evelyn does not play
quite fair. By her request ' on the sudden ' for their
return he says he discovered her marriage. But her
letter is a refusal to part with them ! However, he goes
on to say : ' I faild not to transmitt them to her nor she
to return them, as indeede finding nothing in them '.
Apart from his questionable veracity, he omits to say
anything about the six letters retained by her in June
1674, for the possession of which he was still as insistent
as she was tenacious.

On the ' discovery ' of her marriage, he says he
' resolv'd to live under an affected ignorance ; assuredly
knowing (and as afterwards I learn'd) that this niceness
could not possibly proceede from herselfe ; but from
some other prevalent obligation : and I ever esteem'd it
an impertinence to be over-curious, where I found there
was designe of concealement '. But as Evelyn wrote this
in 1685, is he not being wise after the event ? ' And yet
againe,' he continues more logically, ' when I call'd to
mind, the reiterated promises she had made me, never

---

[1] Evelyn himself.
[2] The only letters from him to her that have survived are copies made
by him.
[3] P. 57.

to alter her condition, without first acquainting me with
it ; I was somtimes in suspence of my conjecture and
would often reproch myselfe for the suggestion '.[1]
That is sufficiently plausible.

In June Godolphin duly carried out his mission at
The Hague. As far as we know, neither his embarkation nor his return the same month called forth any
notice from Margaret. Furthermore, not until their
household was established, did they cohabit. Therefore,
Margaret went on as before the marriage. Evelyn's
visits were not restricted : that might be Godolphin's
wish, indeed it might be another Godolphin touch.
His reserved and cautious temperament made possible
his friendliness to Evelyn. In turn, in later years, he was a
warm supporter of both William III and James II : ' He
had voted for excluding the Duke of York from the
Throne ; he had been that King's Minister '.[2] He
outmanœuvred Evelyn, yet contrived to be his friend.
At the beginning of July there was a further instance of
his determination to keep the marriage secret. For the
week beginning 29th June, Margaret stayed at Sayes
Court : On 5th July Godolphin and the two Howard
sisters joined the party for dinner. After dinner, while
young Mary Evelyn walked in the garden with her
ageing grandpapa, Sir Richard Browne, or played
ombre with him, her elders talked of Lord Berkeley's
projected new appointment. Lady Berkeley, they
said, could talk of nothing else. My lord was going as
Ambassador Extraordinary to France, and (with Sir
William Temple and Sir Leoline Jenkins) plenipoten-
tiary at the congress of Nimeguen. Lady Berkeley had
no desire to leave London, they said ; yet it necessitated

[1] Op. cit., p. 59.   [2] W. S. Churchill : Life of Marlborough, vol. ii, p. 74.

her staying in Paris, and later, moving on to Holland.
It would be comforting to have Margaret with her :
would she not come ? How could they be parted ?
Lady Berkeley had pleaded that they had been such good
friends for two and a half years. Perhaps Godolphin's
opinion was now sought. He would voice approval,
without hesitation, and ruminate : ' an excellent idea,
it will help Margaret to pass this trying period of uncon-
summation. And she would be, temporarily, away
from Evelyn's spiritual sphere '. Evelyn, unable to
understand how Margaret could leave her friends, would
say : ' of course I know she loves Lady Berkeley, and
feels she cannot desert her '. Evelyn would reflect
further : ' Why did I imagine that she was married,
now that I see she can leave Godolphin as easily as
Godolphin lets her go ? . . . But alas, she's leaving me
also ; how I shall miss my Berkeley House visits ! '
Margaret, happy in the knowledge that there would be
no calls upon her acting, and understanding Godolphin's
self-denying approval, would repeat : ' How can I
desert Lady Berkeley ? ' Mrs. Evelyn, in her shy,
attractive manner would murmur : ' Of course not ',
secretly hoping that while Margaret was in Paris John
would spend more time at Sayes Court and taste her
new season's delicious raspberry preserve.

In the evening, the artful, consistent Godolphin
returned to London with the Howards, leaving Margaret
to make the journey with Evelyn the following day.

The next day Evelyn wrote to his wife :

' My deare, I set downe my Friend, and yr child
(for so I pray you now esteeme her with me) at my
L[ady] Sunderlands and went directly to Whitehall :
I believe she is sincerely yours, and being so, you have

the greatest jewell in the world, and at my heart I am glad you love her, for indeed she will make you love God, and our blessed Saviour above all things in this world, and so more and more indeare you to me : she shew'd me a little present you made her, which I find she tooke kindly, and I thanke you for it, 'twas a signe of yr love :

'I dare say she speakes her heart, when she tells me the value she has for you, and askes me, *why I would have a friend, who have so good a wife* : But you know (and oft I have told her) that you yr selfe were the cause of it ; if you call to mind how incessantly you desir'd me to be acquainted with her, I say her in particular, and propheticaly, & often told me, I should thank you for her, and so I do a thousand times, for the greate good which my soule has receiv'd from her piety, prudence, example and prayers both for me, and for you, and which I am sure she continues : she is now yours in spirit and the bond of friendship as she is mine, and how can I be happier ? for if (as you pronounce) there were never two more alike in our way, and inclination, it is not possible you should long converse together, but you must contract something of that which in her resembles me, and so of necessity I must love you more, since resemblance is the motive of all affection ; Be but like her, and you are perfect, make her like you and she will be so ; you both want something of each other, and I of you both, and I hope in God we shall all be the better for one another, and that this threefold cord shall never be broken :

'You designe to see her, and to give her thanks for the honour she did us : I could have wish'd we might have enjoy'd her with perfect quiet, and without

forreine and unexpected interruption as we promised
ourselves : we will not despaire of being so happy one
day, if we live to see her returne from abroad ; for she
is the best natur'd in ye world : her teares to you were
teares of love, such as you sometimes us'd to me, and
therefore I am assur'd she loves you dearly, and thinks
perfectly well of you, and as you indeede deserve :

'Pray let the day you visite my friend be *Tuesday*
next, which is as it were consecrated by us, not for idle
conversation, but to pray, or reade, or discourse of holy
things ; and if you will put up a supplication together,
I know you will both remember the absent, who never
forgets either of you continualy : The Lord Jesus
blesse you : You will likely find her at home iññediately
after dinner, or about 11 in the morning if she be not at
Twickenham. . . .'

Perhaps some comment on this extraordinary letter
is necessary. Margaret's question, 'Why I would have
a friend, who have so good a wife', is a gentle indication
that now Margaret is married, Evelyn's friendship is
unnecessary, an indication, surely not lost upon Mrs.
Evelyn, who must have thought that Margaret was
altogether protesting too much. Evelyn's 'Be but
like her, and you are perfect' signifies Mrs. Evelyn's
lack of spirituality ; 'make her like you, and she will
be so', a measure of Margaret's lack of practical
affairs. 'The forreine and unexpected interruption'
seems to resolve itself into Evelyn's antipathy towards
Godolphin : Evelyn could not have had so much of
Margaret's company at Sayes Court as he wanted. For
nearly three years Evelyn had visited Margaret on all
possible Tuesdays, yet apparently Mrs. Evelyn remained
in complete ignorance of that day's special character.

The letter concludes : ' I believe it will be this moneth or six weekes ere my L. Berkeley be ready to set forth — he goes extraordinary as I told you : we shall be infinitely oblig'd to my dear friend and that family, I cannot devise how we shall deserve it : yet God may give us some opportunity, though we forsee it not, and you know how we both abhor ingratitude.'

The obligation Evelyn refers to was the arrangement for his son John, now twenty years old, to travel with the Berkeleys and Margaret, and to reside with them in Paris. Margaret had agreed to act as his governess, a role for which she felt herself unfitted. Evelyn, though grateful to her, could not approve of her going. In a letter to him in July 1675, her own despondency at the prospect of leaving England is manifest :

' . . . As to your sons being near me which is the thing we last spoke of, I know no good it will be to him unles it be that he has one will be just in relating how well he behaves himself, for what can I advice him to ? have not you told him everything he ought to doe and is he not perfectly good ? : well but still you believ highly of me : I promis you if he be sicke I will take great caer of him, my maid shall wash his lininn, and I will giv him such instroctions as I am able which he, I fear, will have great caus and consequently som inclinations to laugh at :

' You saw me yesterday merey, oh lord how far from it was I, god knows: never any body undertooke a jurney with les inclination, but you will say why doe you go : why only becaus I thinke it is fit for me to doe it, and for no other reason : for I dont dout but I might well be spaerd : I have in this as in all other things of importance begd gods asistance earnestly and often, and I hope I doe that which best pleyses him, sens I folow reason and that he has given to be our guid : your prayers I don't dout but I shall have : I shall need them for my spirets will be sunke down very low and very often too, unles god almighty doe exstrodinarly asist me : I cant call this a perfect afliction, and yet I cant help being troubled at it : god forgive me if it be more then is alowable, though I hope I am perfectly resignd to him :

' Well I wounder peeple desire to live long : never trust me though ther wear no hope of a beter life if I would not gladly leav this tomorow, for if I cant be hapey who realy am for much at my ease, who can if I can not live without croses, who have no children servants master father mouther, things that though they are blesings yet often they prove otherwis, and the best of them have days in which one thinkes one could live without them : but yet I am not hapey absolutly nor never shall I find in this life, for so soon as ever I begin to conclud myself so, that miniut somthing or other coms to cross it and leavs me weary of this life : I own a great deal of this proceeds from the peevchnes and impaitance of my natur, but how much beter is it (unles upon devine considerations) not to be at all, then to be and not to be perfectly hapey, for god knows a litle pain maks one forget a long health, and the unkindnes of one frind maks one forget the frindship of many for a time, for we by nateur are apter to grine then laugh, the first sound we make is crying, our childhood is scarce any thing els but frowardnes, and so but in a litle more reasonable maner we proceed till we dye, so that unles we had hops of a beter world we wear of all things most miserable, for reason is apter to put fears into the mind

wherby it disturbs the man — then [than] hop[e]s wherby
he may [be] comforted :

'I believ you will thinke I keep a great deal of woe
with a little afliction, but this is a day you are to have a
leter and so you bring paitance along with you to the
reading of it I dont dout : excuse my not being at
home for I have today to go to my sisters [1], in but this
therfore pray parden me : . . . god blese you.'

Diffident though Margaret might be, she proffered
Mrs. Evelyn certain acceptable advice regarding young
Evelyn's sojourn abroad :

'I am very glad that Mrs Evelyn dos consider me
enough to take my advice though but in a litle measuer,
it shows she thinks I love her, which is what I would
very much wish she shold be convincd of', is the
beginning of another July letter. Margaret again lets
fall a gentle hint, that her need of Evelyn's friendship
is no longer vital ; 'Pray let . . . [Mrs. Evelyn] se
this and every leter els I writ, for hereafter I will entend
then to you both, sens you are all one and I to you both
a true frind and homble sarvant' She concludes by
telling Evelyn that his estimate of the time before Lord
Berkeley sets out will be more than doubled ; and
displays qualms for her duplicity : 'Pray god blese you
and all yours, you are very humble in ascribing any part
of your goodnes to my example : god knows I am a
wretched siner and nothing but infinet mersey could
pardon my innumerable faults : such a pen never any
body had '.

A few days later in July, Margaret again reveals the
despondency into which she is thrown ; there is no
doubt that to hide the truth from Evelyn is a great

[1] Dorothy or/and Mary Blagge.

burden to her : ' I wish from my soul you would not prais me : oh if you know me : but the les I seem to thinke my self the greater I apear in your humble eye : therefore I am silent '. And again she directs Evelyn to the good qualities of his wife who, by this time, surely surmised that Margaret had tired of the friendship : ' I rejoice in all the plesent hours you spend with your wife, it is my daily prayer thet god would not only continue but still more and more increas your hapenes in her, who is I daer say every way perfectly good and exelent : you know I daer not lye nor disemble, and this is my opinion truly '.

Dare not lie ? What does she mean then, by these words, which occur in the same letter ? ' I am not so near that state of life as you imagin, nor may be shall never venture. I have quite other thoughts, but I am gods, let but his will be done on me in me and by me : your frind will be hapey howsoever or wheresoever I be disposed of.' Evelyn obviously asked if she intended to marry, and this was her answer. No wonder she considers herself ' a wretchd siner ' when her predicament forces her to lie. But her lie must have cheered the disconsolate Evelyn, who already feeling the pang of separation, has sought encouragement from her : this is her reply : ' You bid me incourage you in your duty alas what can I say : ther is for you prais that coms not from man but god : ther is for you an eternal exseeding great reward : you serv your maker and redeemer and asist his poor servant : after this what can any thing that I shall speake signify to you '.

Margaret was so distressed that the most pleasant of all Evelyn's meditations went unread for a few days : ' I have reseved your *Tuesdays Meditation*, and have not

yet had time to read it ', she said in this same letter.
The other three works on the Creation were completed
by the beginning of 1675 : perhaps *Tuesdays Meditation*
was rewritten and thereby delayed. Here is an extract :

'We will now Walk into yonder parterre, and
Observe how these small and despicable Atomes of the
flowry rudiments, are cast into their cold and expos'd
Beds, and rotting (in appearance) under the damp
mould, should yet at last, after so many moneths of
dark and close Imprisonment, abandon'd to the nipping
frosts, chilling snows, and hideous stormes, triumph-
antly emerge, and rallying their small particles, put
forth their pretty and extravagant rootes, serpenting in
the Earth, whose milk and blood they greedily take in,
and as the Season approches, penetrate the Crusty
Surface of the Genial Couch, peeping out first with
a small, pale thried, tip'd with a faint enamell, and
mantl'd in their greene scarfs, which by degrees they
explaine, discovering the raies of a long conceil'd, but
admirable beauty in the leaves, bud, and flower, which
they delicately unfold, unplaiting their tresses, and
modestly un-vailing their virginal blushes, which is
sometimes guarded with vulnerary bristles, and pali-
saded with pungent thorns, 'till being kissed open by the
cherishing Zephires, they are temted to peepe upon the
glorious eye of ye World, ye Sunn, and, as awakn'd out
of their cradles (in which the gentle-Wind had rock'd
them asleepe) raise their drowsie heads, and begin to
vest themselves like so many eastern Queenes : with
what infinite delight, and satisfaction, do we in our
Gardens, behold some of these modest Nymphs open
their chast and fragrant boosomes, at the first dawning of
the fresh morning ! Some we may see halfe dress'd,

K

others yet but in their infant Swath-bands : Some that ye would take to be clad in White Sattin, or figur'd Snow : some in Velvet and cloth of tissue : They are pinck't, plaited, chambletted, embroidred, pennach'd, and chamarr'd with gold ; others againe have ye resemblance of a soft mother of pearle ; they hang their little bells of flexible Saphyrs, and pendents of rubie, others open their painted cups, pretty paniers and boxes lin'd with crimson, and incarnadine damasks ; vasetts of Chrystal, variegated as Achates, vein'd and streak'd with Colours Celestial, flaming and radiant, and of a gemmy lusture ; all of them blooming, all of them faire, and not *one* of them *black*, because they are all innocent : They peepe out of their Vergin buds, as out of so many eyes, trickling into teares of joy, and turning themselves into a thousand varieties, some are erect, others reflex'd, arch'd, round, spiral, pyramidal, wreath'd, jagg'd, escalop'd and indented ; some are single, others double, and curl'd ; tufted, truss'd-up and pursh'd, deck't with plumes of plush, and feather'd tops, crown'd and adorn'd as a royal Bride for the day of her Nuptials. . . .'

Margaret's impending departure hung like a heavy cloud over Evelyn's horizon. Her summer holiday at Twickenham, which began in July, seemed to his shattered spirit a greater wrench than ever. Fortunately, his attention just now was directed to other matters. A law case of old Mrs. Howard and her daughters (for whom Evelyn acted as a trustee) took them to Nottingham assizes on 15th July. The journey through Henley and Oxford proved a pleasant diversion. The University had not forgotten his services in 1667, when he procured for them the Arundel Marbles

JOHN EVELYN
From the portrait by Sir Godfrey Kneller at Christ Church

' when they were not so much as thought of ' ; he now
dined with Robert Spencer in Christ Church, with
Vice-Chancellor Ralph Bathurst the president of
Trinity, and heard in humid July heat the speeches of
the Act. Evelyn's friends, too, were honoured, Bathurst
entertaining them to dinner at Trinity.

Between Oxford and Northampton, Evelyn's party
fell in with Dorothy Howard's lover James Graham, a
suitor not particularly favoured by Mrs. Howard.
Evelyn's advice being sought, he spoke ' to the advantage of the young gent. more out of pitty, than that I
thought she deserv'd no better ' he says ; ' for though
he was a gent. of a good family, yet there was greate
inequalitys '.[1]

The day before the law case came on, Evelyn
delighted in Lord Sunderland's place at Althorp, four
miles from Northampton.

His ten days' absence from Margaret came to an end
on 18th July, when he was back in his lodgings at Bell
Yard to welcome her on a short visit from Twickenham.
Together they received the Holy Communion at St.
James's, and dined at a poor widow's house : the pomp and
entertainments of university and nobility all forgotten.

At the end of the month Evelyn had a worrying
week, when his son developed smallpox ; however,
the young man made a good recovery, and ' ranting
Nanny ' writing with a breath of her usual gaiety from
Windsor hoped that ' his beauty would be as dangerous
to the ladies as ever '. But there must have been some
disfigurement, for an expensive peruke costing ninety
shillings was bought for him.[2]

[1] *Diary*, 13th July 1675.
[2] Evelyn's *Account Book*, 1673–81.

Margaret, writing to Mrs. Evelyn, also sent her sympathy, extended her love again and stated what has been disproved — 'I doe not use to lye' :

'It is a grivious thing that no worldly comfort can com to us without som very unplesant sircomstance atending it : for no sooner did I thinke my self very hapey in finding the kind profestions you made in the garden, confirmd by your hand and seal : but presently I was aflicted at the news of my poor pupils illnes : I am endeeed most exstreamly consarnd for him, but I hope in god his youth will overcom this distemper and your sorow will be turn'd into joy : that this diseas is over before he was oblidgd to leav you who are, I hear, too caerfull of him' : Margaret goes on, with more honesty than tact : 'poor Mr Evelyn has beg'd me most earnestly to make use of my nuw interest in you by puting you in mind that my lady brown ¹ never had the small pox till about your age and your fullnes of blood : but above all, how dear you are to him who can not thinke of parting with you, though he has enjoyd this 23 year your company — so well you have dischargd your duty and so engaging . . . [? has your] maner of living been : . . . With the truthful, engaging admission, she continues : 'I am very ill at expressions though indeed in this case wear I never so able I would not make use of my talent, for though the highest things that one could say would be all true, yet they would sound like what I hate — compliment and disemulation : and doe hope you will except the naked truth with out any art at all, which is that endeed I have a perfect sinsear kindnes for you, as good an opinion of you as 'tis posisable for me to have of any body, and that I thinke Mr. Evelyn

¹ Sir Richard Browne's wife, Mrs. Evelyn's mother.

perfectly hapey in you : this I realy think and when
you know me beter you will find I doe not use to lye :

'I beg you will be so very charitable as to give me
an account somtimes how your son dos who has my
best wishes : and most earnest prayers too . . . pray
let Mr Evelyn know how late it is, and that I thinke
besides one leter from me to one hous is enough at a
time, and pray tell him I shall not se London a great
whill, but above all pray let him know that I wish his
son as I would wish my own had I one.'

Consequently, Evelyn saw little of Margaret during
August ; only on one occasion did he journey to see
her at Twickenham. She mentions no movements of
Godolphin, who probably met her on his Newmarket —
Windsor — Twickenham circuit, and continued to
avoid foreign service. Margaret surprised Mrs. Evelyn
on the last day of the month by arriving at Sayes Court
before Evelyn had returned from a London visit.
Evelyn would be piqued rather than surprised at this
unusual behaviour ; never before had Margaret denied
herself of his welcome. The object of her visit was to
hand him a letter of attorney (illegally signed ' Margarit
Blagge ') granting him power to deal with her financial
affairs during her absence in Paris. Margaret, still intent
on enlarging or dispersing her friendship, allowed
Mrs. Evelyn to accompany her for a part of the return
journey, while Evelyn remained at home disconsolate.

Mrs. Evelyn lost no time in offering her son's
bedroom to Bohun, an offer she was confident he would
accept, or she would never have told him she was
' writing amid the groans of Sir Richard Browne
with an attack of the gout (with an addition of paine
which leaves us doubtful whether stone or winde), the

interruptions of my daughters, the noise of a hammer in the next room and my father's complaints'. She entices him with a description of some recent 'hot venson pasty' when her 'success in the oven was not ill, so that we were very merry at the eating of it, two of the company soaked over a pipe and bottle till eleven at night with great contentment, your company being only wanting and often wished for by them. . . . I fancy you will be very commodiously lodged in Jack's absence both for a closet and chimney, so that you need not be at any expence but resolve to take possession as soone as you & convenience will give you leave.' [1]

In September and October Evelyn resumed his visits to Berkeley House ; indeed in the latter month he spent only six days at Sayes Court, though in this instance, he was under other obligations. The imminence of Lord Berkeley's departure brought him to London on 11th October. A week later Evelyn wrote to his wife : 'I have ben every day since I came up, buisily employ'd, partly among my Bro. Comissrs. and partly about my owne concernes. . . .' (Incidentally, he dined with Margaret on the day of his arrival.) ' On Wednesday ', he continues, 'I went and had my teeth repair'd by Monsr. Gosnell (as you advis'd) and the next day walk'd to Kensington, where my son and I din'd with Mr Henshaw ; [2] but that night such a defluction fell on my teeth, that till this day I have had little or no ease ; but at last it is asswag'd by the swelling of my face : My Ld. Berkeley having now kiss'd the King's hand, and resolv'd it seems to set forwards on Moneday next. . . . Peg [3] came to me yesterday in the evening in a kind of

---

[1] Letter, 20th September 1675.
[2] Thomas Henshaw, F.R.S., a fellow-traveller in Italy.   [3] Margaret.

alarm, to settle her whole affaires in my hands, which
is all don in writing ; and especialy to deplore the
departing from her deare friends among which (I
assure you) she esteemes you one of the first. If it be
possible she will come and see you and Sir Richard one
day this weeke, but will not be able to stay a night ;
and it is in feare she shall be hardly able to come downe
at all. . . .' Evelyn next mentions the financial
arrangements arising out of his son's journey : ' I shall
receive . . . the odd hundred I am constrained to
make use of myselfe to put Jack in equipage etc. . . . I
am going this day to ye exchange, by direction of Sir
St[ephen] Fox (who has a son of his at Paris) to take
order with a French merchant for ye returne of Mrs
Blaggs and Jacks mony by Bill of Exchange. . . . On
Thursday I am to receive all my Lord Ambassrs orders
about his buisinesse, which he puts intirely into my
hands and management, and I know not how to avoyd
or refuse it ; I am likewise to receive and pay a greate
deal of mony for him this weeke, for he will trust no
creature but me ; so that if I be at liberty at all this
weeke it must be towards the latter end of it ; but after
this extreame buisy brunt is over, I shall be I hope at
better leasure to looke after my concernes as well at
home as here.' . . . ' I have not ben at Berkeley
house these 4 daies, I have all this from Peg. . . . I
have given her all necessary instructions concerning
Jack, but she says she must have yours too : If they go
on this day sennight, William [Evelyn's coachman]
must prepare the horses, for it will I find be well taken,
that I grace their traine, at least some part of the way :
but of this you shall have advice.' Doubtless Evelyn
desired to accompany Margaret some part of the way, too.

In relating the London news, he praises a sermon at St. James's given by Bohun, possibly diluting her pleasure thereat by adding : ' all our friends were there from Berkeley house and other quarters '. He concludes in a manner that forces upon us a suspicion that Mrs. Evelyn gave him instructions to impart a detailed account of his London activities : ' Now for Pettycoats : here is very little at this tim : I have seene Lady Tuke twice : At Berkeley house I have eaten twice ; once at Slingsbys, once at Sr Stephen Foxes, and once at Kensington, and so you have the whole history of the past weeke from the bottome to the top . . . the Lord blesse you, and all under your roofe : I will see you as soon as ever I can.'

All plans came near to abandonment on 27th October, when the choleric Lord Berkeley alarmed the Council at Whitehall by a fit of apoplexy. For a few hours everyone, says Evelyn in the *Life*,[1] ' banished all thoughts of embassys, and consequently of our going into France : but God was more gracious, to him '. Gracious to Berkeley, but, apparently, not to Evelyn, if we interpret that intentional superfluous comma. Had he not to part with Margaret, when Berkeley recovered? The time for departure was drawing near, but so good and rapid was his recovery that all arrangements held. There was no escape from separation.

On the 9th November, five days before sailing, Evelyn wrote, from his lodgings in Westminster, to his wife :

' Pray come to Berkeley house after dinner : but Mrs Blagge is not there ; yet it shall go for a visite.[2]

---

[1] P. 60.
[2] This summons was not apparently accepted.

My Ld Berkeley gos on Moneday,[1] and Peg was againe yesterday to tell me, she would if possible waite on you, tho' she would not tell me what day, and says her visite was to you alone, and I had nothing to do with it : however I see her so hurried about that I believe she will at last beg you to see her here, that she may (as she says) kisse and weepe over you : for she is inwardly extreamely sad : If she do come I presume it will be on Thursday or not at all, and if so, I will give you notice, that you be not surprized '. Evelyn then reports the dissembling Margaret : ' she says she has not in the world any friend, but you and I on whom she can realy confide, wh I take very kindly : I have this day sent a letter to Mr Bullack [2] at Dover to provide vessells to transport 40 horses and 4 coaches [3] against the end of next weeke : William must prepare for my accompanying them : I am now seeking an honest Marchant to returne mony by : Peg lay not at home last night, will be all this day with her sisters, tomorrow with Lady Sunderland (who is expected there this night) and then she has onely Thursday to dispose to all the rest : for Friday and Saturday, I believe she will hardly stirr : I think to be with you Friday night : [4] and to meete my Lord and Traine as they go by at New Crosse. . . . I am now going to dine at Berkeley house wth my Lord and Lady onely, and to take their last directions : This is all from yrs.'

With a heavy heart Evelyn sat down to dinner at Berkeley House. Under the prevailing sad conditions,

[1] He sailed on Sunday, 14th November 1675.
[2] Evelyn's deputy for the sick and wounded prisoners at Dover.
[3] In *Diary*, 10th November 1675, Evelyn records ' 3 coaches, 3 wagons, and about 40 horse besides my Coach '.
[4] Evelyn did not manage to get home on Friday, 12th November.

this last meal before sailing was a duty, not a pleasure.
Lady Berkeley fretted at her journey, and feared for her
touchy husband's health. Margaret's absence made the
occasion, for Evelyn, still more poignant. Where was
she? Saying farewell to her sisters, and to ' all the rest '
including Godolphin, Evelyn supposed.

After dinner, Evelyn went home to Sayes Court, to
be ready to drive the next day, to meet Berkeley and his
entourage at New Cross *en route* to Dover.

It was hard, indeed, for Margaret to say goodbye to
Evelyn in her trying circumstances. She had to behave
as though their friendship were intact. Had she not
said that she ' may never venture marriage ' ? Yet she
could not encourage him unduly. As the moment of
embarkation approached, she could not restrain her
tears. Two days' travelling had brought them to
Canterbury : ' after we had ben at prayers in the
cathedral ', says Evelyn, ' she declar'd to me with what
exceeding regret, she was to leave her friends, not
without many teares : I expostulated with her ; Why
she would go then ? I am ingag'd said she, to my Lady
Berkeley who tells me, I breake her heart, if I forsake
her ; and you see in what condition her Lord is ; and,
poore woman, what would become of her, if he should
die, and she have never a friend by her ? ' Of course,
this was the ostensible reason for evacuation. But she
was in a tearful agony of conflicting emotions rather
than in the agony of separation. Accordingly we must
pardon her second falsehood when she said : ' Nor
would I have people think, I retire out of any other
respect : But Mr Evelyn, if ever I returne againe, and
do not marry, I will still retire, & end my dayes among
you '. At which, all Evelyn's suspicions of her being

married vanished, as well they might.

At this point (according to the *Life*), Evelyn believes her tears are shed for himself and Godolphin : ' Do you not think ', he reports her as saying, ' that it aflicts me to the soule to part from you, and from one whom I am sure, you believe, I love intirely ? ' Evelyn is now convinced ' she had left her heart at another place, and with one that therefore did not accompany her ; because he was of as relenting a nature, and durst not trust his passion, whilst their designe was to conceale their relation '. But wisdom after the event will not do ; a little earlier in the *Life*,[1] in commenting on their marriage, Evelyn was persuaded that Margaret and Godolphin ' lived with the same reserves that the angels do in Heaven '. Actually, at this moment, he was in ignorance of their relation. On 13th November the party arrived at Dover, where Margaret handed Evelyn her will. Prayers followed the solemn ceremony. Early the next morning, which was Sunday and gloriously finc, Evelyn ' waited on her againe. . . . I know not how ', he said in the same unconvincing strain, ' you part from your lover ; but never may you feele what it is to part from a friend : I believe there is one you realy love, and that 'tis mutual : How is it then you thus go from him and he from you ? This is strange proceeding, 'tis spiritual ! 'tis high ! 'tis mysterious and singular ; but find it a name if you can, for I confesse, I understand it not : nothing is in nature so repugnant as Love, and Absence, when nothing forbids the object to be present . . . since I know of no ingagement you have to go from your friends, and those whom you professe to love : go back, go back then and be

[1] P. 60.

happy both ; for this course will weare ye both out, if realy you love him.' Margaret cried : ' For goodness sake, do not breake my heart, you see I am ingag'd [to Lady Berkeley], and then she wept, and ware such a clowde of sorrow all that morning, that she could hardly speak a word when I led her downe to the company, now preparing to go on board . . . upon the beach, we tooke solemn leave, and I should discover too much of my weaknesse to expresse the trouble I was in, to see her so overwhelm'd with griefe, that she could not utter one word : but thus she was caryed into the yacht, when being a little launch'd into the sea.' [1]

It is to be regretted that this moving farewell scene cannot be appreciated as it seems to deserve when we recall that Evelyn was writing after the event, and that, at the moment of Margaret's departure (being still in ignorance of her marriage), his knowledge of the emotions that racked her was imperfect. His own feelings were dominated by one of frustration ; inwardly rejoiced that she ' may never venture marriage ', he was deprived by her departure of any opportunity to benefit from her words. Furthermore, the scene is inconsistent with his fanatical opposition to her marriage ; an opposition which remained active for at least another five months, as we shall discover. No ; there were tears of sympathy for the blind and punished Evelyn, tears for Godolphin who had opened her eyes and urged her to this disciplinary voyage, and the rest were for her own unhappy state : all were echoed by the gentle morning waves breaking on the shingle.

[1] *Life*, p. 62.

CHAPTER IX

PARIS

1675-76

EVELYN, perplexed, irritated, wounded, at Margaret's absence, was in no hurry to write to her. If Godolphin hoped to breach the friendship, he had already achieved a certain measure of success ; Margaret received no word from Evelyn for six weeks, and she waited three weeks before she told him of her safe arrival at Paris. On 13th December, she wrote her second letter,[1] which began : ' my frind I have never heard a silable from you sens I cam to paris, which I wounder at a litle, but I take it not ill, becaus I daer say you have a very good reason for it, as you have for most things you doe '. ' I daer say you have a very good reason ' must have touched Evelyn's wound. She continued : ' I promisd you an acount of our jurney: ther was nothing in it exstrodinary, no ill accedent, nothing like pinto travaile [2] we wear not above seven hours upon sea : pray let me know how to derect a leter to you without troubleing any body els with them : I have seen nothing sens I cam to Paris but the hous[e] I lye on, and shops which I thinke I live in, for I have hardly bin ever out of one sens I cam, not upon my own acount, I asuer you : by the way, but I am so sleepey I cant writ one word more : we must stay till morow.

---

[1] *Life*, pp. 64-5, with omissions and alterations.
[2] F. M. Pinto, *Peregrination*, transl. 1663.

'Well now I am upe and awake, and now I finish what last night I begun : I have just bought your son a new suit of cloths, very gentil and fin, and today we begin to learn french together : he is to learn to dance also, which truly I thinke is very necessary for him : he is a very good husband of his mony and of his time, and I hope you will not repent his coming hither : he talks much more then he usd to doe, and is very chearfull as ever I knuw any youth in my life, and as inosently merey as 'tis posiable for any body to be : we are to learn arithmaticke, in fin we entend to grow very wise :

'My lord Berkeley holds well to a miracle, mends a litle every day, nothing of his deseas remains but shortnes of breath upon coming upe stairs : . . .

'I have had very litle time to my self sens I cam hither, which aflicts me most exstreamly, but I hope I shall have more : there has bin a prist to viset me, but without vainety, I thinke I said as much for my opinion as he did for his. I am now reading mon : claude [1] *defence de la reformation*, and like it most exstreamly : you need have no fears for me, god knows the more one sees of ther church, the more one finds to dislike in it : I did not imagin the tenth part of the suppersteon I find in it : yet still I aprove of ther orders : the monesterys are very holy institutions, if they be abusd that is not ther fault what is not perverted : mariage it self is grown a snaer, and peeple fear to dispos of ther sons yong for fear the remedey increas the diseas : but when I have comended that bait of thers, I have said for them I thinke all that can be said, and I thinke that any reasonable body can say :

'Pray let . . . [Mrs.] Evelyn know the post is hers

[1] Jean Claude. The book was published in 1673.

and [that I should] like to be troubled with a leter : if
I . . [knew] what was nuw or improved sens she
was hear I would indeaver to make my leter plesent by
a discription of the maner of it, but fearing I shall but
giv an acount of what already she knows, I will content
my self with a relation of what I am sertain she is very
well aquainted with all, which is her son : I love him
mightely, he is so good and so very even and cheerfull
in his temper, and maks me laugh when somtims I am
ready god knows to cry, for peeple can have spleen in
paris, let them talk what they will of the aire, that I asuer
them well : dear Mr. Evelyn god blese you and all
yours. . . .'

Evelyn eventually recovered from the initial shock
of Margaret's absence. By the end of January 1676, his
perplexity forgotten or effaced, he had written seven
letters to her three. It was not easy for Margaret to
keep tally, and, occasionally, she failed to answer some
of Evelyn's questions. He therefore instructed her to
number her letters : thus, rather pertly, she heads the
letter of 28th January : 'Jan the 28 my 2 leter sens I
obeyd your orders : this in awswer to your 7 leter
dated the 2 of Jan : now I hope you are pleysd'.

The change from Berkeley House seems to have
improved the style of her letters, they are more secular,
sane, businesslike, as this one shows : and she will not
allow Evelyn to interfere in her work as governess to
his son :

'. . . as for your son I believ he will easily comfort
himself for his being shut out of biusnes, but his wretched
horse troubles him more then any thing : it being still
starke blind, and lame into the bargain : endeed it has
cost him a great deal of mony in phisicke and peeple to

atend him, and I fear he will never get a farthing for
him, so that he will be disapointed, not only of the
mony you said he shold get by it, but he will suffer the
los of what the Jade has cost him, so that I thinke a litle
present of ten pound would not be unwellcom to him,
but he knows nothing of this request of min truly, nor
I believ will he ever aske for mony, though he shold
realy want it :

'I beg of you not to writ to him to change his
studys, nor to put so many things upon him at once, for
it is imposiable he can prophet by that way ; but let him
be well verst in one thing first, and after that he may
proceed to more : for this is the ready way to spoil him
and let him know nothing throorly, but talke of many
things, which I would not giv a rush for : this is Mr
Benson's [1] opinion as well as min I asuer you ;

' As for your leters to my lord I suppos he has them,
but he never speaks to me of any that he has had : all
that I beg of you is to make them as short as you can,
for the poor man dos fret at a long leter most wounder-
fully much, I thinke you had best writ them to my lady
for she has more time, and not quit so hasty : I read that
part of the leter that consarnd him aloud : he bid me giv
you many thanks for your caer and that for the spec-
tacles he did not need them : . . . and so dear frind
farwell pray god blese and keep you save and defend
you in all danger and adversitys now and for ever.'

Mrs. Evelyn had greater faith in Margaret's common-
sense direction of her son's studies than in Evelyn's
didactic : 'You are so good to those I love,' she writes
to Margaret, ' and particularly to one who needs your
dayly advice, that I cannot but acknowledge you are

---

[1] A friend of J. Evelyn, jun.

infinitly kind, Jack cannot faile to obtaine any request
he makes to you, and wee will not see farther then is
necessary why it is made, with an implicit faith wee
submitt to you, and without saying any more then
truth I had rather follow your councell then any person
I know, Jack is perfectly yours by inclination as well as
in compleance to his fathers and my desires. I am not
affraid you have charmed him, but assured he has perfect
respect for you . . . as he ought to have for so perfect
a friend.'

We have noticed that Evelyn quickly recovered his
epistolary output to Margaret. But he had no confidence now that his efforts were welcome. In July, a
few weeks after her marriage, Margaret had declared,
rather airily, that she would write once or twice to him
while she was away — a much less generous ration than
that she actually served. Of course, in July, with Godolphin's advice still ringing in her ears, the need to dis-
courage Evelyn seemed rightly urgent. Now she felt
she could relax her unfriendly, restrictive attitude.
Time, or her sweet, forgiving nature, had softened the
blow. In her fourth letter from Paris, dated 4th
February, addressed ' at Mr Fountaine a merchant near
London Stone ' (not to trouble anybody else) to his
eighth, she says : ' your leters are never too long dear
friend, and how can you be so unkind as to believ I
could be capable of saying once a month was fair for
you to writ to me : endeed were I able to be angary with
you I would be it upon this subject '. In discussing
Godolphin, she is wary and evasive : Evelyn, putting
out a feeler to ascertain her attitude towards her lover,
remarked on his virtues and suitability, to which
Margaret replied : ' As for S[idney] being good I dout

L

it not, as for his being worthy of me I believe him not only that, but worthy of anybody.'

Describing Margaret's stay in Paris in the *Life*, Evelyn emphasizes her lack of time for spiritual exercises, quoting, but only in part, the rest of the letter : ' as to my soul alase I have no time : I am weary of my life I swear : cards we play at for 4 hours every day, who ever coms to my lady [1] I must be by to interpret : wherever she gos, if my lady hamilton [2] be not at hom, I must go : so that poor I can scarce say my prayers, seldom or never read : dear frind pray hartly that if it be gods will, I may be restored to my own peeple, god, and nation : for though god be every where, I can not call upon him as I can at home : therfore for godsake pray that I may quickely be restored to the congregation of gods peeple and to the precence of my dear frinds : whom as my life I love :

' What doe you mean by doeing exstrodinary things ? I could content myself with any thing I thinke now so I were at home again, but I must doe nothing rashly : I hope in god by your prayers and my own firm resolutions which I have taken, to return as soon home as ever I can quickly to se you, and therefore leav woundering : all the day I am so wearyd here with perpeatuly dedecating myself to peeple that at 11 a cloke, when your son and Mr Benson com into my chamber, I cant posiably denigh myself the satisfaction of seting and talking with them an hour or so : which when I have don before I can get to bed 'tis near one a cloke, so that in the morning the soonest I rise is 8 a cloke which I bestow in an hour

---

[1] Lady Berkeley.

[2] Hamilton, Lady Frances Jennings (1648–1731) : sister of Sarah, Duchess of Marlborough, wife of Sir George Hamilton, afterwards wife of Richard Talbot, Earl of Tyrconnel.

for prayer and splams [*sic*] and an hour and half for reading, somtims one booke somtims another : then I dres, then to pub[lic] prayers : then din then talk : then at three pray publickly again then talke : god knows till 6 a cloke then pray for you and som more then play at cards till bedtim oh pity me.'

If Evelyn meant spiritual incitements by his ambiguous phrase ' exstrodinary things ', the prudent Margaret commented : ' I must doe nothing rashly '. She proved to be less discreet in saying that she would return home ' quickly to se you therefore leav woundering ', for it evidently inspired Evelyn to one of his more passionate flights : [1]

' If my wishes to see you, my delight to heare from you, my continual thoughts of prayers for yu be symptoms of Love, I cannot helpe it ; you have given me an heart, and carried away another, and wedded me wth a ring, and obligd me by a Sacrament of perpetual Friendship, which every Tuesday I solemnly renew in ye communion of Saints, even that intire office, wth very little alteration, your prayer for G—— [2] I religiously joyne, and I am with yu in spirit, and I rise for ye most part refresh'd : and if yu will believe me, welcome the return of that day, as if it were ye Lords, for yu are ye cause I dedicate much of it to him, and that, but since I knew yu, and yr zeale to serve him, I have been more carefull and dilligent to serve him also, tho wth many more infirmities : O my Saint, how will you shine in heaven ! what a Circle of starrs will crowne her [*sic*] head, what Jubily must the Angels do yr cause, who still go on to fill up their number, and repaire the losse of

---

[1] A part of this letter was utilized by Evelyn in the *Life*, p. 105.
[2] Godolphin.

those who fell from their Integrity :

'I protest yu are ye joy of my heart, and I have thoughts above this world most as I consider your glorious progresse, yr effectual example, your happy successes, and the fruite that has ben planted by yr holy industry and labour of love amongst many here : Do I discharge my fancy ? or my duty, in acknowledging my selfe infinitely indebted for much you have taught me : Surely I do not flatter, when I write this, but in ye presence of God, I blesse his name, and magnifie his Graces in you ; Go on excelent creature in ye holy path, and leade mee after you : Be it by yr beauty, by yr witt, yr conversation, yr prayers, and devotion, yr zeale, holy insinuation, example yr charity and peculiar addressess, being wily you catch them by craft, and be a fisheresse of soules : what shall I add, dear friend ? yu are fortunate in all yu set yr hand too, because you lay out all yr perfection in workes of God, the winning of soules, and a greate is yr reward :

' Often I have considered it, and how God has prospered you and by a peculiar providence conducted you thro many passages and dutyes : or shall I ascribe it to your prudence, ever prudence is ye gift of God : The pension which yu sold, how timely was it suggested by him ; it had now ben at an end, or in greate danger, and yu had lost £1200 : the £500 which by our honest stratagem, you have recovered, when it was in no security is another instance of Gods care of yu : I know yu often ponder these things, and I praise God for them with you, and heartily I have besought him, that nothing of yr concerne may ever miscarry by my counsell or conduct : Your interests I make as much my owne, as if you were the child of my owne bowells, I rejoice when

yu rejoice, I weepe when yu weepe, O that I were also
of ye same mind, for then I should be allways in heaven,
where yours is : In a word I unfaind'ly love yu for yr
piety : I looke upon yu as ye servant of ye Lord Jesus,
and sorry I am, to have been of late so unprofitable to
you in ye way of devotion, and then so many of my
lettrs have so little relishd of ye Good you expect from
me and for which I believe you endure I should at all
write to yu : O that I had a quill of that dove which
inspires all our thoughts, sanctifies all our intentions,
guide our hands recording his praises, & fills our hearts
with heavenly joy & our mouths wth [illeg.] :

'I am often considering whether I shall evermore see
yu in this world : The time is short, 'tis uncertain, &
when I shall see you I am still in danger of losing you
againe : [1] therefore ah, how I often think to be where we
may meete, and here part for ever, & clasp yu in ye
boosom of oʳ Lord : You are young, have longer to
live, & farther to go, but yet are nearer home & to that
repose by much than I : You are already in ye porch,
I hardly in ye way, you made hast by times, I set out
late, tho you came after me, far is my frind before mee :
quicken me then that I may mend my pace, or rather
O Lord do thou quicken mee.'

It would be enlightening to read Margaret's reply
to this emotional appeal (wherein we notice, in the
matter of Margaret's pension, Evelyn confuses his own
acumen with God's guidance), for the like of which we
have to go back to the spring of 1673. No answer,
unfortunately, survives. She would certainly be embarrassed, and find it irksome, distasteful, to respond.
Probably she disregarded it altogether ; or possibly her

[1] By her marriage to Godolphin.

letter of 28th February may have served as a *riposte* :
' this leter is to be short becaus it is only to let you
know I have reseaved all your three leters sens I writ
any thing in awswer to you, but this post I have no
maner of time, next tusday you shall have a perticuler
acount of all things : you shold have it now but endeed I
can not now for the bell is going to ring and I cant say a
word more, but that I am yours with all my hart '.

All in all, Evelyn derived no pleasure from any
aspect of Margaret's absence. He was discontented at
Lord Berkeley's treatment of his son, who, being lodged
in a high cold garret next to the footmen, without
hangings or furnishings, felt unable to entertain visitors.
My Lord perhaps showed contempt for young Evelyn's
social qualities, and in consequence relegated him to the
attic. ' He will never dance, nor make a legg well, nor
have his perriwig or cravate in good order, or be *à la
mode*, but he will prove an honest sollid, and judicious
man, and be very good company.' [1] Such was my
lord's testimonial. Mrs. Evelyn, too, felt her son's
position to be ignominious : ' I am sorry Jack is no
better used ', she wrote to Evelyn, ' by the Lord
Am[bassador] after so many professions of kindnesse,
let him be never so great he is not too good to treat
people cevely according to their quality, the honour of
his family obliges Jack to be much more galant than if
he were upon his own account, and therefore spares
your purse the lesse, it is a nice point to medle with and
yet me thinks my lord should not be faithfully served
and complemented by you for slighting your sonne. . . .' [2]

The presence of Margaret was young Evelyn's only

---

[1] Letter to Evelyn, 27th May 1676.
[2] Letter to Evelyn, 31st January 1676.

consolation and he was deeply disturbed when arrangements were made for her return to England : ' I
should have passed my time very ill ', he writes to his
father on 25th March, ' if I had not the happinesse of her
conversation sometimes, which has bin the only circumstance that has made my being here tolerable. She is
now going from hence, which puts me into extream
melancholy to think of parting with my governesse, so
good a governesse, and so excellent a friend as I have
found her on all occasions. Pray sir consider that I am
left here alone for now she is out of that family I cannot
indure the thoughts of it and if I should put my self into
it agen I am sure I should dye with melancholy in a
little time all that I have any value for in France goes
away with her. All her virtues all her charms, her piety
and her goodnesse to me assault me all at once. . . . I
am become most desperately her humble servant.'

He then inflicted, unknowingly, upon his father a
distressing pang : ' That man is too happy who is to be
master of such a treasure. . . .' In a letter to one of his
sisters, he described Margaret (perhaps because she
allowed herself a necklace of pearls) as his ' pretty,
pious, pearly governesse '. So little did he relish
remaining in the Berkeley household without her, he
implored : ' Either let me come home and settle to the
law or let me travel '.

It is true that Lord Berkeley was well served by
Evelyn. The former said : ' You cannot do anything
to displease me '. Bombarded by thrice-weekly appeals,
he spent the greater part of each week soliciting the
same tardy Treasury officials (who, a few years earlier,
denied him shirts and money for the prisoners of the
Dutch War) for his lordship's salary and ' extraordin-

aries ' : ' So often suffering ', he says, ' the being brow-
beaten by the Earl of Danby then Lord Treasurer to
that degree, as to be asked in reproch, whether I were
my Lord Berkeley's steward ?   All which, with a servile
assiduity (and a long and anxious waiting on his thres-
hold) I endur'd weeke after weeke, winter & summer.'[1]
But despite Evelyn's efforts and trials, money remained
overdue, and the ambassadorial plate found its way into
pawn : to be followed by more appeals for money to
redeem it.

Lady Berkeley made use of Evelyn the virtuoso and
only wrote to him when she wanted something : a
remedy for the piles or alterations for him to supervise
at Berkeley House (so doleful with the shutters up) :
wainscoting to be installed in the manner of the Duchess
of Cleveland's (but without her expensive inlaid cedar
or walnut) and ' three very pritty chimney backs of
iron ' to be chosen by Evelyn for her ladyship's bed-
rooms and dressing-room.

[1] Letter, Evelyn to Lady Sylvius, 4th November 1688.

CHAPTER X

THE MARRIAGE
CONFESSION
1676–77

AT the end of March, Margaret left the Berkeleys and
Paris for England, accompanied by Bernard Grenville, [1]
a Groom of the Bedchamber who, having served as an
Envoy Extraordinary to the Duchess of Savoy, was on
his way home from Italy : an escort probably arranged
by Godolphin. In the *Life*,[2] Evelyn would have us
believe that Margaret's departure was an escape from
the profanity of the Berkeley household, from the
' interruption of her assiduous course and devotion'.
That may well be so, but laden ' with a world of fine
petticotes',[3] her decision to return coincided with
Lord Berkeley's orders to proceed to Nimeguen.[4] In
any case, Margaret's feelings at her homecoming must
have been confused. However distasteful to her the
Parisian social round, equally disturbing was the thought
of her impending confession to Evelyn of the marriage ;
in fact, since May 1675 it had never been lulled for a
moment.

In Paris she could procrastinate for ever ; in England, confession, sooner or later, would be inevitable.

---

[1] Or Granville, 1631–1701 : father of George Granville, Lord Lans-
downe.   [2] P. 66.
[3] Letter, J. Evelyn, jun., to his sister Mary, 10th April 1675.
[4] He did not, however, arrive until November 1676.

157

Would she find it any easier to confess now, eleven months after marriage? In the previous May her friendship for Evelyn was still ruled by her heart. Thus, unwilling to injure, she could not break off at an instant, though she withdrew without explanation. If her head had been in command, she would have kept nothing back. Now that she was used to the idea of marriage and her heart unquestionably Godolphin's, would confession be any easier? Could she not recall to Evelyn his advice of June 1674 that she should marry? No; that advice had been pretty thoroughly cancelled by Evelyn's subsequent behaviour. And if his only surviving letter to Paris is a fair example of the tenor or temperature of his later behaviour, it continued to make confession difficult for her.

On 3rd April Margaret landed at Dover. There is no record that Godolphin welcomed her, but he may well have done so. However, in no great haste to meet Evelyn, she coolly deferred advising him of her arrival until she came to London on the 6th, when she arranged to meet him the following day. His *Diary* entry is reticent: 'Came my dearest friend to my great joy, whom after I had welcomed, I gave account to of her business, and returned home'. For the next few days there were reunion dinners and suppers. Margaret, Lady Sunderland, Mrs. Graham, and Mrs. Howard dined at Sayes Court, and Evelyn supped with Margaret at Lady Sunderland's. On 26th April Evelyn dined with Margaret at her new lodgings in Mrs. Warner's house in Covent Garden; Margaret's erratic sister, Lady Yarborough, was also present. To anyone conversant with Lady Yarborough's character [1] it will be

---

[1] See A. Hamilton, *Memoirs of Count Grammont.*

no surprise to learn that she divulged the secret of
Margaret's marriage ; she was born to let the cat out of
the bag. No details of this dramatic scene have come
down to us ; but we may visualize the fluffy Lady
Yarborough chattering, inconsequently, to Evelyn and
Margaret about Godolphin, when the word 'husband'
suddenly slipped out. After a moment's dreadful
silence, Evelyn, trembling with anger, would ask
Margaret : 'Why didn't you tell me you were married ? ' Lady Yarborough, serious for a moment,
would ask Margaret's forgiveness for her thoughtless-
ness, and then, breaking the tension with her irrepress-
ible laughter, would say : 'The marriage had to be
revealed ! Why not by me ? I'm as good a revealer as
anyone ! ' And her laughter would echo long after she
left the tearful Margaret to explain her secrecy as best
she could.

The shock, which to Evelyn must have been shatter-
ing, and so embarrassing as to have kept him out of the
Coffee Houses, is glossed over in the *Life*.[1] He speaks
only of 'friendly expostulations' between Margaret and
himself, 'for the unkindnesse of her so long & indus-
triously conceiling from me the circumstances of her
marriage ; because she had express'd her sorrow with
such an asseveration, as in my life before, I never heard
her utter — so as I could not but forgive her heartily ;
nor did this suffice ; for she often acknowledg'd her
fault, and beg'd that I would not diminish ought of my
good opinion of her to the least wounding the intire
friendship which was betweene us : protesting, she had
ben so afflicted in her selfe for it ; that, were it to do
againe, no consideration in the world, should have

[1] P. 67.

prevaild on her to break her promise, as some had don, to her regrett'. The allusion here is undoubtedly to Godolphin and Lady Berkeley, on whom Evelyn puts the onus, because Margaret, he says, ' was a lady of so *exact* and nice a *conscience* : that, for all the world, she would not have violated her promise ; nor did I ever find it in the least, save *this* ; which (when all is don) was of no great importance ; save that I tooke it a little to heart, she should so long conceale a thing from me, who had so earnestly advisd her to marry. . . .'

Yes, Evelyn advised her to marry, but only in the summer of 1674 when there seemed little risk of his advice being accepted. Practically in the same breath, he had opposed the alternative retreat to Hereford, advising her to ' stay as she was '. When she reasserted her desire to go to Hereford, he gave way ; but Lady Berkeley, probably acting under orders from Godolphin, stepped in, and persuaded her to remain at Berkeley House.

It will be remembered that Margaret's distracted letters during the crisis implied that she hardly knew whether she loved Godolphin for himself, or Evelyn and God. However, Godolphin's eyes were opened, and in those summer months, behind a screen of secrecy, he re-courted Margaret. His success was gradually revealed in Margaret's ' worldliness ' which he nourished during her holidays with him at Twicken-ham. Evelyn, in his attempted sublimation, reduced Margaret to a pale and lean ghost of her former self ; under Godolphin's care she blossomed into a wife. This was the metamorphosis that shocked Evelyn, and which, surely, Margaret now had to expound.

When Evelyn said : ' Why didn't you tell me you

were married?' Margaret we imagine replied, in
effect: 'Despite all your unrelenting efforts to keep me
celibate, I fell in love again with Godolphin. After all,
he'd been expecting me, waiting for me, for nine years.
Thus I failed you. It was this failure that I could not
bring myself to confess. For I felt that such a failure
amounted to a revolt from your precepts. And I had
broken our pact of friendship. You know how weak
a creature I am, how sensitive a regard I have for you:
so I was forced into silence. My visit to Paris enabled
me to avoid you for a while: it was Godolphin's idea.
Time is a wonderful healer, and I hoped you would hear
of the marriage from other lips. For I had no courage
to tell you.'

What answer may we read in Evelyn's heart?
Should he not say: 'My saint! What have I to do
with this? Have I failed? Surely not. I tried to keep
the love of Heaven in your heart: what more could
I do?'

Is not this utterance, this attitude, consonant to the
quoted meditations? He desired to translate Margaret
into a saint; her later letters and marriage spell his
failure to do so. His disappointment in her will yet be
further manifest, by another chastisement written after
his knowledge of the marriage. Furthermore, she had
rejoiced his heart for nearly twelve months, with the
lie that she 'may never venture marriage'. In consolation, he continued to sublimate her and, later on, her
memory, by writing her life, not as fate decreed (as we
have noticed) but as he would have us to see it. Accordingly we read in the *Life*,[1] Margaret desired that he
'would continue to assist her, with those little services

1 P. 68.

she was pleased to accept', and that on 27th June, moving from Covent Garden, she 'formed her pretty family at Berkeley house (now empty) . . . and began to receive the visits, and usuall congratulations upon marriages, so universaly approvd of'. Thus Evelyn would have us believe that all was well.

The house-warming happened to coincide with the anniversary of Evelyn's wedding-day, forcing upon him a hard choice under new and trying circumstances ; he decided, however, to dine with Margaret.

It is worthy of notice that although Evelyn saw Margaret on several occasions before she left Covent Garden, and resumed his weekly visits at Berkeley House as soon as possible, he did not pray regularly with her until 14th August ; and then followed this with a remarkable consistency until 20th September : for a parallel in such mutual piety we have to go back as far as the early months of 1674.

What had happened ? What was the significance of this intensive devotional sequence ? To answer the question, we must first attempt a fuller diagnosis of Evelyn's feelings immediately after hearing of the marriage. The imaginary initial scene, already depicted, probably gave way to anger and frustration, for he would not easily forgive Margaret's lie and her violation of the pact — put the blame on whom he will.

Yet his anger could only have been transient. His exacerbation could not have lasted many weeks (though it was to flare up again, as we shall see). His real and deep feeling for her could not be shattered in a moment of anger. With religion as its basis, the friendship held fast, though perhaps on his part with some show of resignation ; in fact, we may believe the friendship not only held fast, but reasserted itself, in a manner reborn, and for the first time since its inception, modulated into love and became perfectly disinterested.

It seems that Evelyn expressed his willingness to free Margaret of all her obligations under the pact of friendship. To this offer she replied : ' As to your freeing me of all my promises I thinke myself much oblidgd to you for trusting me : be asuerd it shall not be don the les for my having liberty for so long as you love god I shall love you '. He decided to take her at her word.

He now began to practice the precepts of his friend Jeremy Taylor,[1] remembering that 'when you admonish your friend, let it be without bitterness ; when you chide . . . let it be without reproach '. Perhaps this reproof also went home to him : ' He that gives advice to his friend and exacts obedience to it, does not the kindness and ingenuity of a friend, but the office and pertness of a school-master.' Too often had Evelyn disregarded the words : ' Give thy friend counsel wisely and charitably, but leave him to his liberty whether he will follow thee or no : and be not angry if thy counsel be rejected '.

But Evelyn also could discourse on friendship. In his new inspiration, he proceeded to do so, and began writing for Margaret *Œconomics to a newly married friend*, the inaptly named testament of their newly aligned association. He began by acknowledging the ' improvement of his spirit ' derived from Margaret's example, zeal, and Christian life, and that Friendship ' opens the heart '.

He set out to show her ' what obligations ' there might still lie upon her to continue their friendship and

---

[1] *Discourse of the Nature and Offices of Friendship*, 1657.

'not to think any new condition or circumstance of life' of force to absolve her from the protestations made at the Altar of Friendship. He says, in his new fervour : 'There is nothing more active, free, and disinterested than a real friend', and 'one hour's conversation with a well-chosen friend is more profitable than a year of meditation'. That is well-nigh akin to self-immolation. He repeats that their friendship is where it was, and her marriage 'alters not the case'. He pronounces it 'indissoluble'. 'Did you not calculate for all events ? ' he asks her, 'and that to come, and were ye not then as fully determin'd to make him yours ? Do I pretend to disturb his right, by justifying my owne ? ' and quotes a portion of one of her early letters : 'Deare Friend, never was any creature ty'd to another in such bonds of friendship as is my heart to you : may our love last as long as life ; and if there be a love to you, or me, when we shall see the God of Love : O may you be my companion in those blessed abodes, where we shall without any imperfection, serve our perfect Lord : Amen with all my Heart'. Evelyn adds : 'I say so too'.

> For I not for an houre did love
> Or for a day desire
> But with my soule had from above
> This endles holy fire.[1]

Thus he might well have declared the immutability of his love, before he went on to advise her on conjugal affairs. 'Fix the love and affection of your husband at the very beginning of your coming together,' he writes, ''tis a rare thing to find a restless and unjust passion turned into a calme, constant and equal love, after 'tis in possession of its desired object, because the

[1] H. Vaughan, "A Song to Amoret."

imagination is always so much greater than the fruition.
But his, and yours, being determined and sanctified by
better principles will flow in an even stream and altogether unperturbed. The morose and churlish may be
won by the conversation of their wives, modesty of
their attire, the sweetness and decorum of their graces.
Only the charms of virtue are permanent and lasting.
The graces of Love never preserve their innate and
genuine worth but through the noblest of our senses,
the eye, and the ear.' Then follows a striking passage,
in which Evelyn anticipated Pater : [1] ' Beauty and
youth are gifts of nature and they are amiable and
powerful, but they are not Love's object, because they
have no real consistence. Before they receive their last
finishings they are not perfect, and when they are at
their height and flower (even at that instant) they
decline, and nothing in this world stands the same a
moment.' He analyses masculine infatuation, although
there was no risk of it in Godolphin's protracted court-
ship : ' Tis certain that that which young men most
admire in your sex, is brittler than chrystal, fading as a
blossom, it lasts for a little season, looks prettily, and is
safe whilst 'tis only looked on, but every touch sullies
its lustre, and before it bears it even falls away, and
many times the admirer's affection with it, because he
makes an idol of a phantom, and dotes upon a thing
which has no being.' He also gives advice on more
practical matters, servants, charwomen, home skill in
physic and surgery, distilling cordial waters, the use of
Schroder's or the *London Dispensary* published by N.
Culpeper, Wiseman's *Chirurgerie*, and the knowledge
of herbs. He tells her : ' never should you be without

---

[1] *The Renaissance* : conclusion.

M

Venice-Treacle, Mithredate, Diascordium, Lucatello's
Balsome, Bez[o]ar, Gascoigne's or Lady Kent's Powder,
Irish-slate, conserve of roses, Diapalma and such
common and necessary Electuaries, Salves and cordials
as are continually in use in families, especially in the
country'. He advises upon everything : land tenure,
tillage, pasture, the wife's legal status : ' for marriage
entitles . . . [the husband] to your person, and to all
you bring with it of worldly goods, and he can do with
it what he pleases without your consent'. His remarks
on the difficulties of raising and educating children are
obviously based on his own trying experience : ' I
know and remember myself, what pretty chimeras,
castles, and ideas virgins and batchelors are wont to
form to themselves, what they will do, and how they
will govern their families, educate, and institute their
children, before they have either ; and the resolution
is commendable, the speculation diverting, but the
practice not quite so easy'.

It is pleasant to picture Evelyn imparting his advice
on all these things to Margaret at Berkeley House and
saying to her : ' You do not dance, nor sing by book
and tableture, nor play on music, . . . I would neither
have daughter or son too accomplish'd in them: as far as
tends to graceful carriage of the body and refreshing the
spirits, I think is more than commendable, 'tis necessary:
it is sufficient that your children dance the courants,
touch the theorb, lute or harpsicord, and sing to time,
but 'tis not necessary they should compose, play at
first sight or dance like comedians.'

Then remembering his wife's accomplishment, he
adds : ' To paint a miniature is a sweet diversion '.
For classical learning he recommends the ' Lives of

Plutarch, Cyrus, and such of the Roman or modern
stories as are extant in French or English, but especially
the Morals of Plutarch, and those excellent pieces of
Seneca, Antoninus, Epictetus, and of the poets Virgil
and Juvenal.   More than this ', he continues in the
strain that Pope sounded in 1711,[1] ' unless it be a very
great more, is apt to turn to impertinence and vanity.'
Indiscreetly, he harks back to the crisis of 1674, balancing
the virtues of virginity against the advantages of matri-
mony, and throws up an uncommon sidelight on
Godolphin : Evelyn considers Godolphin's busy life
at Court and abroad a discouragement to Margaret ;
' less busy might his life have been had he been either
half so prudent as you or so early instructed and so
sincerely '.   One more extract must be quoted that
gives us the philosopher Evelyn : ' The pleasures of
life make a man not one grain the better for them, so
little does the exercise of the body profit farther than
what it contributes to its health, and to the sustaining
of the fatigues of the spirit '.   If Margaret failed in the art
and practice of marriage, it would not be Evelyn's fault.[2]

   With the resuscitation of the friendship on such a
basis during the summer of 1676, Evelyn's anxiety
would come to an end. Now that the marriage, always
threatening, had taken place, and the pact remained
unaffected, there was no fear, no restraint : Margaret
could freely respond to Evelyn's new disinterestedness,
and certainly with Godolphin's approval.

   No wonder, then, that throughout these summer
months Margaret remained in London, and for the

---

[1] *Essay on Criticism.*
[2] Two pages of the Œconomics are in B.M. Add. MS. 15950 : printed
in Appendix B of *Life.*

first time since the pact felt no desire for a holiday at Twickenham. In such halcyon days that charming place shook off its character, for Evelyn, as Margaret's hideout, and resumed in his mind its normal attraction as a resort.

Of course, the Godolphins' stay at Berkeley House could only be temporary, contingent as it was upon Lord Berkeley's absence at Nimeguen ; his health might determine a sudden return. A more permanent home was therefore sought, and found, in an apartment just over against His Majesty's woodyard by the Thames-side leading to Scotland Yard which, in September, Evelyn undertook to repair and adapt. What a labour of love it must have been during the ensuing months to devise with Margaret ' that pretty habitation . . . which ', he says, ' she contriv'd. with so much ingenuity '. Robert Hooke, the inventor, architect, and member of the Royal Society acted as a surveyor for them.

Godolphin, still attached to the Court and the King at Newmarket or elsewhere, could safely leave the choice of furnishings to the excellent taste of Evelyn and Margaret. What joy to go to Lambeth together to choose marble fireplaces, and perhaps order looking-glasses at the Duke of Buckingham's glass-works ! There was greater joy for Evelyn at the end of September : while Godolphin attended the King at Newmarket for racing and hawking, Margaret stayed at Sayes Court for three weeks to see the bronze and green autumn foliage and to taste and admire Evelyn's rare, aromatic, French pears, now in full bearing. He told her of the calamus with which he intended to be-flag the moat, of the sweet willows he would plant upon the banks, and the bulbs and jonquils he wanted from France. As it was, the garden was sheer delight. In the orangery, the last tuberoses were still pearly white, fragrant and tenuous amongst the orange trees newly housed for the winter. There was fun on the bowling-green, and quiet talk in the garden until the evening mist sent them in to supper. Margaret teased him for calling this paradise his ' poor quiet villa '.

Young John Evelyn recalled his only pleasant memories of Paris with his ' pretty pious pearly governess '. In the study, Evelyn showed her his *scrittore* of prince wood, the drawing of Louis XIV by Nanteuil, and the fine black cabinet with the secret drawers which he brought back with him from Italy. It was pleasant, too, to renew her acquaintance with dear faithful John Strickland, Evelyn's bailiff, as sturdy and well-rooted as any of Evelyn's trees. In the Library, Margaret admired the Barbadoes cedar table of one huge plank six feet broad and nine feet long, and the orderly arrangement of the books (although she could not find those she wanted because Evelyn's catalogue stood in need of re-writing). Perhaps she wondered at the luxurious library furnishings, at the chairs and cushions and folding stools all in green glossy silk. Most imposing of all was the long cushion in cloth of gold embroidered with Evelyn's arms.

The October visit to Sayes Court gave Margaret many opportunities to show her regard for Mrs. Evelyn ; Margaret doubtless insisted that she should accompany herself and Evelyn on the 9th to Blackwall to see some Italian curiosities, and on the 17th again her presence was desired when they all dined together at Berkeley House. These concessions also reflected

Evelyn's new magnanimity. But he often had Margaret to himself during this month, particularly when they dined together in celebration of the pact on the 16th, and of his birthday on the 31st.

Now that jealousy, the error of excess, was eradicated, Evelyn could continue to idealize Margaret with no hint of fanaticism, his spirit rapt in pure and exquisite passion. She, too, was happy. Her soft, gentle nature was revitalized with a new self-possession, and she could say to him with simplicity and sweetness : ' As long as you love God, I shall love you '. Their friendship, their ΑΓΑΠΑ, would be everlasting ; with Evelyn newly re-qualified for his self-appointed name *Philaretes*, it could not be otherwise.

Evelyn, as usual, had other interests and duties. His many secular services to Margaret and her circle were still further increased by his labours for the Berkeleys ; he supervised the Twickenham estate accounts, and obliged Lady Berkeley in the packing ' with mats ' of the great tapestries of the story of Francis I, which, at the end of 1676, were sent to Nimeguen with her red velvet chairs ' sticht with gold ', leaving the hall at Berkeley House drab and colourless.

As a former Lady of the Bedchamber, Lady Berkeley was entitled to a New Year gift from the Queen ; the receipt of which placed her under another obligation to Evelyn. Her Ladyship, with something of her husband's impecuniosity, thus thanks him : ' I am very glad you tooke ye New Year's gifts of the Queen in money : I hope you demanded for 2 years, 2 Christmases being past since I came away '.

According to Evelyn,[1] Margaret lived more or less

---

[1] *Life*, p. 69.

in retirement with Godolphin during the winter, avoid-
ing society and hospitality as much as possible. Godolphin's own movements are as elusive as ever, though,
on one occasion, he attracted attention. Just before
Christmas he delighted the boyish heart of King Charles
and earned his sporting approbation for the skill and
daring with which he drove the dangerous horse-
sledges on the frozen ponds of St. James's.

Margaret and Godolphin were foils for each other ;
she adored him, who possessed all the qualities that she
herself lacked. Yet he could always rely on her judgment. Her piety leavened his love of gaming, her
softness his composure. If she were retiring, he was
buoyant, perhaps a trifle jaunty. She was fashioned for
the life spiritual, he for the temporal. She was graceful,
he ungainly and, in early manhood, slight as a jockey.
But although Godolphin was continually attached to
the Court, he, like Margaret, had none of its moral
failings.

They were a supremely happy and ideally matched
couple when, on hearing that Lord Berkeley was about
to return from Nimeguen, they moved into their new
apartment near Scotland Yard on 31st March 1677.
Margaret, in returning thanks on 11th May to Mrs.
Evelyn's offer of help in domestic art, wrote to Evelyn :
' I must always take kindly suer your constant desires to
oblidge me, and am very glad I shall be instrocted by so
wise a woman as Mrs Evelyn, whos judgment—no disprais
to you — I would as soon rely on as yours . . . as to our
litle family, aight is the number we are to have nor more
nor les, three dishes of meat at diner we would willingly
have, and no supers at all, no coach doe we entend
to keep but he [Godolphin] has always two riding

horses. . . .' Mrs. Evelyn duly initiated her into the complexities of housekeeping, setting out Godolphin's yearly allowance of £500 in specimen bills of fare, wages of servants, and cost of household goods.[1] Thus, says Evelyn, she settled ' with that handsome and discreet œconomy so natural to her : never was there such an household of faith, never lady more worthy of the blessings she was (in all appearance) entering into, who was so thankful to God for them '.[2]

[1] See *Life*, pp. 223-30, where Mrs. Evelyn's instructions are printed in full.   [2] *Life*, p. 69.

CHAPTER XI

CONCLUSION
1677–78

WHATEVER social obligations were laid upon Margaret
by her marriage, she did not allow them to restrict
Evelyn's weekly visits : apparently she agreed to his
plea that 'no new condition or circumstance' should
absolve her from the obligations of the new interpretation of the pact, and allowed him an average of four
visits a month during her first three months at Scotland
Yard.

One of Evelyn's last labours for the Berkeleys, who
were expected home in June, involved the purchase of
cows, on Lady Berkeley's instructions, for the family
milk supply : 'I would be glad ye baily [bailiff] had as
much as will for ye present buy 2 or 3 or 4 cows against
wee come home which I hope will be very soone'.

In June the Berkeleys returned. Evelyn received
their grateful thanks for his immense trouble, and
recorded that he was 'delivered from that intollerable
servitude & correspondence ; I had leasure to be somewhat more at home, & to myselfe'.[1] If this last observation is to be taken literally, it undoubtedly derived,
partly, from the knowledge that Margaret would not
be at Scotland Yard during the summer months ; in
fact, we lose sight of her, and he paid her no visit
between 3rd July and 18th September : almost certainly

[1] *Diary*, 24th June 1677.

173

she must have warned him of her intended absence. Godolphin was at Windsor with the Court in the middle of August ; otherwise the whereabouts of the couple at this time are unknown ; perhaps so far as the Court allowed, they were on honeymoon. On Evelyn's word that Margaret lived more or less in retirement during the past winter, not until the summer of 1677 did she have an opportunity for a honeymoon. Thus Evelyn admitted, not without a little sadness, that he ' had leasure, to be somewhat more at home, & to myselfe '.

The pleasures of Sayes Court or of Mrs. Evelyn's company were not, apparently, the distraction he sought. After twelve days at home he spent the last fortnight of July visiting his brother George at Wotton, the Duke of Norfolk's ' sweet villa ' at Albury, the rector of Shere, and his son's late tutor, Ralph Bohun (temporarily at Abinger). For the greater part of August he divided his time between Sayes Court and the Duke of Ormond, Lady Ossory, Lord Brouncker, the Earl of Peterborough, and Lady Mordaunt. From 28th August until 14th September he was the guest of Lord Arlington at Euston (where ' the mutton is small but sweet ') and visiting, with his lordship, more nobles and notabilities at Bury St. Edmunds, Thetford, Ipswich, Harwich, Newmarket, Audley End, and Bishops Stortford. After three days at home, he was off to London on 18th September to dine with Margaret : his usual routine was resumed. Mrs. Evelyn sulked excusably for two months, and remarked to her friend Bohun : ' Mr Evelyn has taken his pleasure at Wotton and Euston ',[1] lamenting that she had not dined

[1] Letter, 19th November 1677.

outside Deptford for months. A certain slyness and
subtlety crept into her letters to Evelyn when she felt
neglected : she would say ' were it not business that
keeps you I would murmur at your stay. I hope you
are well and find friends to eat with ', knowing how
well he was faring. Then, endeavouring to arouse a
little envy in him, she would refer to ' the good company we had ' at Sayes Court, when ' you were wished
here by all '.[1]

It is remarkable that after her marriage was made
known, Margaret found little necessity to write to
Evelyn ; at least, only four letters have survived. Of
course, with all conflict and indecision ended (subject
of so many earlier letters) and the friendship apparently
newly founded, occasions for correspondence would
doubtless be infrequent. After her removal to Scotland
Yard, Evelyn received only one letter from her for six
months. On 22nd September 1677, a few days after
she returned from her holiday, she wrote thanking him
for a lengthy *Office* he had written for her, and sought to
impress upon him that ' all this pains ' had been taken
' for no other end then that god may be glorified '.
She made a point of saying that his labours, his ' pious
thoughts and holy order of heavenly devotions ' are
not for herself but for her ' poor frinds ' : quite
markedly, she put her thanks in the plural. In the
Life,[2] Evelyn quotes (with a few adjustments) the
following portion from this September letter, describing it as a benediction written on 31st March immediately after, and for her happy arrival at Scotland
Yard. But we may well prefer to regard it as her
thank-offering — as indeed it was — for the beneficial

[1] Letter, 20th May 1681.   [2] P. 69.

176 JOHN EVELYN AND MRS. GODOLPHIN

honeymoon with Godolphin : ' Lord when this day I
considered my hapines in having perfect health of body,
chearfulnes of mind, no disturbance from without nor
grife within, my time my own, my hous quiat, sweet, and
prity, all maner of conveniance for serving god in
publicke and in private, how hapey in my frinds,
husband, relations, servants, credits and non to wait or
atend upon, but my dear and blesesd god from whom I
reseive this, what a melting joy ran thrugh me at the
thought of all thes mercies. . . .'

Two remarkable occurrences now took place. On
the following day Evelyn visited Margaret and prayed
with her. Although he continued thereafter to visit
her, he never prayed with her again, at least, there is no
record in the *Diary* that he did so. And on 16th
October, the anniversary of the pact, he dined with
Godolphin alone. Whether this strange celebration of
the sacred day explains, or is a sequel to the first, we have
no certain means of knowing. We cannot but be
curious to know why Godolphin was mysteriously
present, and we are especially inquisitive as to what
passed between him and Evelyn : but we can only
conjecture. Did Godolphin at long last object to
Evelyn's praying with her, and decide so to inform him
at the anniversary dinner ? That might well explain
Margaret's absence from the table. It is unfortunate
that there is no clue in her letter of 16th October
(written not only as an anniversary act, but in recompense for her absence) towards any elucidation of these
strange events ; but Evelyn [1] quotes only a portion :
' I thank Almighty God, who has ben so infinitely
gratious to me this yeare : for he has brought me back

[1] *Life*, p. 70.

into my owne native country in safty & honorably :
prosper'd me in my temporal affaires, above my expecta-
tion : continu'd my health, & my friends : deliver'd
me from the torment of suspense : given me an
husband, that above all men-living, I value : in short,
I have little to wish, but a child ; and to contribute
something to my friends hapynesse (which I most
impatiently desire). . . .' Margaret's simple statements
must not be overlooked. She does really mean that she
values Godolphin above all others. Consequently, she
wishes to contribute something to Evelyn's happiness,
implying that now she is happily married, he is unhappy,
or, alternatively, he is unhappy because he has prayed
with her for the last time.

We cannot be certain that Godolphin learnt the
nature of Margaret's letters written to Evelyn before
the marriage. The meditations in her keeping would
still be embarrassing ; she was too sensitive a creature
to endure them locked up in distasteful secrecy :
Godolphin had only to ask a question as to the form
of their praying together, or to be allowed to read
one of the less disinterested passages, to justify his
asking Margaret to put an end to them.

There is one such passage which Margaret could
never have kept under lock and key ; it appears in
An Office for the Lord's Day.[1] If she allowed Godolphin
to read it, the events of 23rd September and 16th
October are perfectly clear and logical. If he confronted
Evelyn and asked for an explanation of the following
confessional, Godolphin, the potential Lord Treasurer,
must have needed all his suavity and control. These

---

[1] P. 65, a later version of the same *Office* written before Margaret's
marriage.

qualities, however, doubtless prevailed, if we take
Burnet's word that 'he had a clear apprehension, and
dispatched business with great method, and with so
much temper, that he had no personal enemies'.

'. . . But as I have wounded Thee by my sinns ;
so hast thou wounded me by thy Love ; Ah that with
Thomas, I might now touch Thee ; not with his hand
as if I doubted ; but with his Faith confessing Thee
when he adored Thee his God & his Lord, and with
inviolable Fidelitie never afterwards doubted, nor for-
sooke thee to the Death : To the Death then will I love
Thee O my Saviour, who hast loved me when I hated
Thee ; and can I doubt thou wilt now disdaine me
coming with a broken and penitent Heart, and with
Teares of Love, to bath thy wounds and mingle them
with thy blood ? No my Jesu, Thou hast given thy
selfe to be Flesh of my Flesh and Bone of my Bone,
God incarnate " Imanuel " God with us — O mysterious
Union ! O Love Unexpressible, and altogether astoni-
shing ! What shall be able to separate my Heart from
Thee — Love stronger than Death — I am espous'd to
one Husband, and desire to present him a chast Vergin ;
for I have vowed to be onely Thine O blessed Bride-
groome of my Soule ! To how many Lovers have I
yet ben prostituted ! To the World, to the Flesh, to
Satan himself and shamefully departed from my first
Love, Ungratefull, disloyall wretch ; and yet thou
sentedst after me, offering me gracious conditions, and
promis'd, that if I would returne, thou wouldst receive
me into thy boosum. O Thou fairer than the Children
of Men ! Lilly of the Vallies, Thou Lovely of ten
thousands ! Nothing is immaculate, nothing is pure,
nothing worthy to approch thy Holiness, but what thou

clensest & purifiest & renewest. . . .'

This anger, this last flagellation, this lapse of Evelyn's act of sublimation was probably written in the summer of 1677 when he was tortured at the thought of Margaret on her honeymoon. Whether it formed the basis of a melodramatic scene, with Margaret on her knees, crying : 'I will be purified, I will be renewed !' and actually caused their readings of meditations to cease on 23rd September we cannot be certain, but it could certainly never promote them. In any case, they came to an end. Evelyn's next visit to Margaret would have been due a week later on 30th September ; as already stated, he did not, however, call at her house except to dine alone with Godolphin on 16th October, sixteen days overdue. Therefore, if his angry lapse created any rift, it may also have prevented his normal visits of 30th September and 7th October, and, furthermore, caused Margaret's absence at the anniversary dinner on the 16th. Ominously, too, her letters to Evelyn (except for two written as late as August and September 1678) now ceased. Perhaps she had become too 'worldly'. As her metamorphosis became more perfect, as she progressed from theopathic rapture through celibacy, conflict, and indecision, towards 'worldliness' and the self-assurance begot of marriage, so her letters became less worthy, in Evelyn's eyes, of preservation. Any written criticism of his lapse would at once be destroyed. In any case, the alchemy of love now directed her letters to Godolphin, who, alas, destroyed them. Can we blame him ? Perhaps he felt that the words she wrote under the pure and steady light of love were for himself alone.

But Evelyn could not have long remained under a cloud : Godolphin would see to that. Throughout the

autumn and winter of 1677 his prayer-less visits to
Margaret went on without further interruption. In
November, he characteristically supported Sir Gabriel
Sylvius's choice of ' ranting Nanny ' Howard for a wife ;
Sir Gabriel being over forty years old (and about to sail
for Holland), Nan twenty-one. But Mrs. Howard
only parted with her daughter out of England because,
says Mrs. Evelyn, Sir Gabriel ' is in so good a station for
honor and profitt '.[1] Nothing escaped Mrs. Evelyn.

Evelyn dined with Margaret on 4th December, and
did not see her again until 8th January of the new year :
we therefore lose sight of her for a month. On this
occasion she was probably out of town on a short farewell holiday with Godolphin, who was due to take up
an appointment in January as Envoy Extraordinary to
the Duke of Villa-Hermosa, governor of the Spanish
Netherlands.

Margaret did not have long to wait for her wish for
maternity, expressed in September, to be fulfilled. In
early January she believed that her child would be born
in early September ; in February her joy was beyond
doubt.

Meanwhile, Godolphin returned from the continent
at the end of January to share a few happy days with her,
before he sailed again, in February, with instructions to
William of Orange that the English Parliament was
unlikely to finance any further the war with France.
He remained near William for a few weeks, returning
home in March. On 4th April Evelyn entertained
Margaret, Godolphin, his brother Sir William Godolphin and their sisters at Sayes Court. By the middle of
April, Godolphin was back again (thus living up to his

[1] Letter to R. Bohun, 19th November 1676.

reputation) with the Prince of Orange, this time staying
five weeks. On 16th May Evelyn commemorated
Margaret's wedding-day by giving a dinner-party for
her and the newly wedded Lady Sylvius and her sister
Dorothy (now married to Colonel James Graham).
Did Evelyn's thoughts revert to the triumvirate in the
ante-chambers of Whitehall ? Ah, those happy days
of ranting Nanny and *The Legend of the Pearle* !
How distant they seemed ! Even his first, exciting
visits to Margaret and her pretty oratory were like
a dream.

In the *Diary* he says this ' was the last time that
blessed creature ever came to my house, now being
great with child, and seldom stirring abroad '.

Before his last visit to The Hague, Godolphin
decided that during his absence, Margaret would need
a friend at hand, perhaps in case of an emergency.
Accordingly, in his official correspondence to Henry
Frederick Thynne — a secretary in Henry Coventry's
office in Whitehall — Godolphin enclosed letters for
her, or when stress of duties prevented his writing,
directed Thynne to convey to her the reason why there
was no letter. We may regard this arrangement as one
of expediency for a speedy delivery to Scotland Yard.
Thynne, however, was something more than a postman;
he was instructed to regard Margaret as his ' charge ',[1]
and, presumably, to keep a protective eye upon her.
Perhaps Godolphin—or Margaret—passed over Evelyn
for this service because he had forfeited their confidence
that he was qualified for such a role.

On 24th June Godolphin landed at Harwich, and
rode in haste to Whitehall and his beloved Margaret.

---

[1] Coventry Papers at Longleat, vol. xli, *ff.* 464, 487, 503.

A month later he purchased the Office of Master of the King's Robes — a step on the road to authority.

We must now return to the question of the tempo of Evelyn's friendship for Margaret. After his lapse of September 1677 and his final act of prayer with her, there is only one indication (apart from the constancy of his weekly visits) that the two friends may have subsequently agreed to the conditions urged by him in his *Œconomics to a newly married friend*. This is seen in his readoption of the sign ΑΓΑΠΑ, spiritual love, with which the last *Office* he wrote for her, is marked. It is for *Trinity Sunday & Octaves after Pentecost*, completed on 8th May 1678, and to which he appended the words, ' The end of ye annual private Offices ' ; as was to be expected, it contained only normal devotional matter, bringing his surviving total of closely written octavo pages for Margaret to more than fourteen hundred.

Doubtless he still worked at the *Œconomics*, intending to present it to her, but her acceptance of this final *credo* of his friendship is not certainly known. Perhaps she considered that neither party had been sufficiently disinterested to justify its acceptance.

Margaret made her last public outing five weeks before her confinement, crossing the river to Lambeth with Evelyn and his wife to see Ashmole's library. Her little dinner-parties went on into August. On one occasion Godolphin assisted her to entertain Evelyn and his wife, and on another, Margaret had Mrs. Evelyn and Lady Mordaunt to herself ; one of those friendly, intimate afternoon gatherings to which only experienced mothers are invited. Apparently the last letter of any substance from Margaret to Evelyn has suffered mutilation ; it is endorsed by him ' An heavenly letter concerning the vicissitud of ye things & enjoymts of the world ', and described by him [1] as a postscript, which, in fact, it does not seem to be. All that he wanted us to read is as as follows : ' . . . [portion torn off] doe is to pray that gods kingdom of grace being erected in our harts, his kingdom of glory may succeed, and so we for ever be with our lord, which endeed I long for more then for all the satisfactions of this world, for ther is no plesuer in this world to be chosen for itself. Eating is to satisfy the pain of hunger, sleep to eas wearynes, and divertisments are to take of[f] the mind from being too long bent upon things that it can not always atend without great inconveenece to the facultys of it : then retyerment again is to eas it of thos burthens and stains it has sustaind and contracted by being in company, so that our wholl life is, in my opinion, a search after remedys, which doe often, if not always, exchange rather than cuer a deseas, but yet I know god has given us many blessings which, if our natuer wear not very depraved, we shold much rejoyce in, but we make so ill use of most of them, that we turn thos things to mischief which are given us for our good : as to the comunion . . . [portion torn off — perhaps with a reference to Godolphin] for I am assured it is for his sake : I am very sory to hear Mrs Evelyn has not bin well, I hope in god she will recover, for what could you doe without that exelent creatuer, pray god of his mersey continu that blesing as long as your life, for methinkes you are mighty hapey in her: god of his infinet mersey bles you both.'

Naturally enough, perhaps, Evelyn saw Margaret

[1] *Life*, p. 74.

only four times during the last three months ; doubtless she was often out of town. Towards the end of August, in bright and genial weather, he ' took his leisure ', calling on the Duke of Norfolk at his palace near Weybridge, Lord St. Albans at Byfleet, and (with the Duke), paying a visit to the Court at Windsor. Having returned to Weybridge, Evelyn went on to Sheen to dine with Henry Brouncker. After dinner, in the fine August afternoon, he walked to Ham House, belonging to the Duchess of Lauderdale, calling, on his way back to London, at Sir Henry Capel's place at Kew to see his excellent fruit trees. After one day at home, Evelyn was back in London arranging with the Duke of Norfolk for the transfer of a portion of the Arundel Library to the Royal Society.

It is difficult to resist the feeling that despite the resolutions in the *Œconomics* Evelyn had been for some time out of touch with Margaret. In fact, we feel that her friendship for him had almost diminished into indifference, and that his interest in her marriage had waned. We are not surprised that his visits were curtailed, but why should her letters become so infrequent ? The phrase, ' The end of ye annual private offices ', breathes an air of finality. His wife's advice and company were preferred before his ; of course, as Margaret's lying-in approached this was to be expected. Yet there was an unmistakable coolness in a letter written to him, in August :

' . . . pray doe me the faver to call in £100 out of claytons [1] hands for my use, who have at this time ocation for it : I shall be very glad to se Mrs Evelyn when she coms : and of my frindshipe you may always rest

[1] Sir Robert Clayton.

asuerd, let the apearances of the contraery be what they will : pardon this morsell of paper I have not a scrap more in the hous : I am with all sinsearty yours.'

So Margaret was still his friend, but with little of the former rapture. She had neglected him, of late, in all ' apearances '. Under those circumstances, not only would Evelyn's passionate flights be frowned upon, but he would be given no opportunity, except in the *Œconomics*, to demonstrate the inviolability of his friendship ; in fact, we are forced to conclude that the theory was never again put into practice.

On the morning of Tuesday, 3rd September, Evelyn [1] called to inquire after Margaret's health, and finding her in labour, stayed until she was safely delivered of her child : it was ' a lovely boy '. Two days later, in Margaret's chamber, the child was christened Francis (after Godolphin's father). Soon afterwards Margaret became very ill : Godolphin was recalled to return with all speed from Windsor. On Sunday, the weather being excessively hot, her illness increased, and when Evelyn was attending the morning service at Deptford, he received an urgent note from Godolphin : ' my poore wife is fallen very ill of a feavor, with lightness in her head & ravings : you know who says ye effectual fervent prayer of a righteous man evayleth much & ye prayer of faith shall save ye sick : I humbly beg your charitable prayers for this poore creature, and your distracted servant.'

Evelyn and his wife immediately went by water to Whitehall, and on arrival at Margaret's house, found her to be suffering from what we would now call

---

[1] In the *Diary* he says he went to dine ' according to his custom every Tuesday ' ; but he had not dined with her for a month.

puerperal fever, accompanied by the most heartrending
delirium. Mrs. Evelyn stayed to give whatever help
she could, and returned to Sayes Court. The next day
Evelyn wrote to her : '. . . distracted beyond all . . .
we here, every moment expecting when this blessed
one should expire : so soon as you were gon, she fell . . .
presently into one of her deliriums, Dr Lower [1] & Short [2]
being [with] her ; yet prescribing nothing save Cordials, so soone as they had well examin'd the breaking
forth of those pimples, which as yet had onely invaded
her neck to some degree : I staid 'til about nine a clock
when she seem'd to take some repose ; but just as I was
going into bed (about 11) was sent for to talke with
Dr Chamberlaine,[3] who (upon yr recomendation) was
call'd for ; But he finding none of the Doctors there,
and seeing now all her back very full of those risings,
would by no meanes direct, without some other Doctor,
tho' otherwise (being fully perswaded the Midwife
(to whom I perceiv'd he was no friend) had left something behind that might be the cause of these malignant
Vapours) he would have don something : Upon this, I
sent for Dr Needham [4] (our Friend) both the other
absolutely refusing to come out of their beds, it being
now neere two a clock : The good Doc[r] came, rising
out of a Sweate, but when he had seene the poore
Creature, was altogether averse from ordering any kind
of thing, the malignancy of the distemper being (as he
sayd) so high & dangerous ; & indeed they were both
agreed that there was no safe medling ; whatever they
should prescribe for one thing, being so repugnant to the

---

[1] Dr. Richard Lower (1631–91).   [2] Dr. Thomas Short (1635–85).
[3] Probably Dr. Peter Chamberlaine, D.Med. Padua, Fellow Coll. of
Physicians, 1628–59, d. 1683.   [4] Dr. Gasper Needham, F.R.S.

other Accidents : so as besides a *Frontal* [1] of Red rose cake, Vinegar, & nutmeg ; they would direct no more ; but leaving her to Gods mercy intended to call againe this morning at eleaven a clock : In this interim the two first Physicians (Lower & Short) appeare, and find not onely all her back, downe to ye wast, but all her breast to ye navil exceedingly inflam'd with those pimples, as thick & fiery as you can possibly imagine, the pidgeons [2] being changed, & blisters (which run abundantly) dress'd, they are likewise departed without anything at all don, but with purpose to meete Dr Needham, & Chamberlaine at the houre apointed : In this Interim, the poore Lady has after very small, and . . . restlesse . . . accesses of raving . . . convulsion, that one may heare her cry . . . to ye farther part of Whitehall, as far as . . . of this nature is capable : so as it grieves our very hearts to be neare, and yet without greate strength & company, there is no keeping her in the bed : when she is out of one of these, she sinkes into profound silence, & wonderfull patience, feeble pulse, scarse perceptible ; and in one of these, I feare she will go away : so as I can see very small hopes from any Crisis, but rather that she grows worse & worse : The poore man [3] being allmost dead with griefe, & lying for the most part flat on ye boards, which he drownes with his teares, begs of me to stay : for that he is not able to speak to ye physitians, & is allmost besides himselfe : I have mony for their Fees, & have already given Dr. Needham & Chamb. each 2 Guinneys : & now at the 3^d consultation (which I presume will be the last) we shall see their utmost resolution : the case I find being

---

[1] Applied to the forehead.
[2] Generally applied to the feet.   [3] Godolphin.

desperate : My Lady Mordaunt has sent *Dr. Fabers* [1]
Aurum potabile ; but none of these Methodist Physitians
value it, nor will advise it ; notwithstanding Mr Godolphin has sent to Parsons Greene for yᵉ Doctor who
makes it ; & who, it seems, is there : Dr. Ridgley [2]
(whom they much rely upon) being out of Towne :
I have not ben in bed at all since Saturday ; but find
myselfe very well in health, I blesse God : I am affraid
I shall conclude this letter with the saddest newes, who
write it by snatches, being continualy call'd away upon
some occasion or other ; the rest being so tired out :
I do not know whether you will think convenient to
make a step up or no, & take yʳ farewell of the most
excellent Creature in the world, & the most worthily
lamented : I cannot dissemble myne infinite griefe for
her, to whose virtue & friendship in particular, I have
ben so greatly obliged ; but this Tragedy teaches me
how vaine it is to set our hearts on any thing in this
world ; There is nothing in it Consistent ; & happy,
thrice happy those who have . . . and early for . . .
better : They are very [mise]rable, who have any
Friendships or attachments to which they cannot frame

[1] Albertus Otto Faber, a German physician ; came to England at the
request of Charles II : In *De Auro potabile medicinali*, Lond. 1677, he
describes *Aurum potabile* as a medicine ' made of the body of gold itself,
totally reduced, without corrosive, into a blood-red gummy or honey-like
substance, such as will yield into Spirit of Wine, and tinge or dye the same
with a high ruby-coloured tincture, of which one ounce being put together,
with sixteen ounces of another convenient liquor, makes up an A.P. or
potable gold, fit to be administered to the most infirm bodies. First
famous in the reign of James I, by Franciscus Antonius, physician of
London. It had cured dropsy, fevers, quotidiana, bloody flux, vomiting,
scurvy, gripings and looseness, White's and Fits of the Mother, and
pleurisy.'
[2] Not mentioned in the *Life* ; Aubrey sent Anthony Wood Dr.
Ridgley's cure for deafness ; see A. Powell, *John Aubrey and His Friends*,
p. 188.

themselves to part with, when God thinks fit to deprive them of them : Now I am waiting for ye Doctors & then shall send Tom [1] to bring you a sad relation, unlesse God be infinitely gracious to our prayers.

' And so (as I feared ;) The Physitians (physitians of no value) they came, but it was too late ; she was now raging afresh ; & with that impetuosity, that the good man himselfe, no longer able to heare or beare it ; with the silence, tho' (I cannot say) consent of the doctors, gave way that the famous (I must now call it something else) *Aurum potabile*, was given her ; The Apothecarie in ye meane time sent home, with a prescription of theires, w^h was onely a forme, & to signifie they confess'd little : Imediately after she had taken 2 or 3 sponefulls of ye Aurum, her raging & convulsion abated ; she wept aboundantly, & thence falling into the Agonies of Death, departed this miserable life, & is now an Angel in Heaven : my teares suffer me to say no more, you will think it is because I truely cannot say enough to describe a losse, that is not to be express'd; for I am in sorrow unspeakable :

' And now here is another sceane that would draw pitty from y^r heart ; to behold the disconsolate, shall I say the miserablest man in ye world ; her Husband, with those miserable Comforters, his brother & sisters,[2] none of them able to beare up against this torrent ; the consequences of which are so distracting, that there is no Creature in the House who either gos about anything, or I thinke minds what is necessary to be don ; either with the Corps, or ye poore Child, or any thing else ; I believe therefore you would do a greate act of

---

[1] Perhaps one of Evelyn's servants.
[2] Sir William Godolphin, Penelope Godolphin, and Anne Godolphin.

Charity to make a step here tomorrow, to assist these people . . . hands so . . . destitute of any solace . . . discreete person . . . who may counsel, & [advise] them in this conjuncture ; This they acknowledge . . . & tacitly wish for you, to raise them . . . up : I am for my owne part confounded also, & begin to be weary & to desire solitude, that I may also bemoane my selfe a little, before my time also come : Do what you think fit : for we are sad Creatures. Never was there such a Tragedy on ye suddaine ; pray be resolved to do them what Charity you can on this occasion, & overule them as to the child for they think not of it.

' I have spoken of ye Apothecary (who prepares that water of Dr. Willis,[1] & is an extreame honest man) to bring it tomorrow that you also may speak with him : I have no more to add, but to desire Tom may go imediately to James Ellis [2] who has not don one stroke of worke here all this whiles, & I know not why.

' The Lord Jesus blesse us all, & ah that I were where my Friend is, for she is hapy, her part is finish'd.

' At 4 in ye Afternoone : She departed just at halfe an houre after one.' Thus, despite all nervous strain, lack of sleep, and the heat of that unusually hot September afternoon, did Evelyn complete his letter.

Godolphin was overwhelmed by his tragic loss, and completely shattered with grief. Evelyn, tired and sorrowful, went home, he says, to spend two days in solitude and sad reflections.

Let us consider the nature of his reflections. In bringing the last painful scene before his wife's eyes, he

---

[1] Probably Dr. Thos. Willis (1621-75) the famous physician ; he discovered the medicinal value of the Adstrop (Oxfordshire) water.

[2] Probably a servant of Godolphin.

had been a comparatively unmoved reporter : perhaps
for her sake he made a conscious effort not to appear
unduly moved. He was a little too detached again, as
he was at the Fire of London. Insensitive as ever, a
further hardening process had now set in, fortifying his
resistance ; he was now as little sensitive to his loss as he
had been in his blindness and detachment to endeavour
to deprive Margaret of earthly love. He could look
upon her death as a sequel to his rejected spiritual love.
Or, penitently, he looked closely into his heart and
reflected that he had a great deal to answer for. He
might even realize that he tried to come between her
and her love for Godolphin, that he was the cause of
all her indecision, of her desire to retreat to Hereford ;
he would acknowledge that he had been blind to her
problem, blind to her tenderness, and that he would
have treated a tender flower with more care. Hereford
might have proved a warm shelter for her, where she
would have thrived — except that his cultivation had
gone too far ; she knew that Hereford could be no
refuge because he would never cease to tend her. So
her only hope was to marry Godolphin — and yet —
there were signs that she was too tender for the open
ground, for the world, for marriage ; and his friendship
would not have killed her. Whatever the bias of his
reflections, Mrs. Evelyn, with wifely tenderness, tried
to console him, and said : ' Remember all are not gone
that love you, and that you still have some who require
your care for them : they would be comforts to you
would you receive them so '. And, to ease his burden,
she charged the midwife with mortal carelessness.

In the *Life*,[1] Evelyn tells us that Margaret, having a

[1] Pp. 79-82.

premonition of her end, had left a letter for Godolphin,
settling her affairs ; ' in case ', she wrote, ' I be to leave
this world, no earthly thing may take up my thoughts.
In the first place, my deare, believe me that of all earthly
things, you were, and are the most deare to me ; and I
am convinc'd that no body ever had a better, or half
so good an husband.' She also expressed her sorrow
for her imperfections, gave directions for various
legacies, and asked to be buried at Godolphin in Cornwall, among her husband's friends. ' Now, my deare,
God be with thee ; pray God blesse you and keepe you
His faithful servant for ever . . . and do not grieve too
much for me, since I hope I shall be happy being very
much resigned to God's will, and leaving this world
with, I hope in Christ Jesus, a good conscience.' Evelyn
says he himself was mentioned at the foot of the letter,
as ' the depositary of her trust, as I was the distributor of
her bounty '.

To soften this inconsiderable mention of himself,
and to inflate our estimation of his share of her heart, he
is forced, at this point, to refer to her having said ' she
knew nothing she had more to wish for in this world,
but that she might do him some signal kindness '. It is
true she wrote in this strain when they ceased to pray
together twelve months before her death, and in consequence Evelyn was obviously unhappy. He goes on,
in the *Life*, to say this wish of hers was made known to
Godolphin, who observed it by ' allowing me the
honour of his friendship & accepting my little services '.
Still inflating our estimation and consoling himself, he
continues : ' for the rest, I have a diamond he gave me
to weare in remembrance of her : and the picture which
she bestow'd upon me her selfe [it will be remembered

that he asked her to sit for it], more lively drawn upon
the table of my heart, the Idëa of her vertue, never to
be worn out : besids a thousand expressions of a
religious & noble friendship under her owne deare
hand, which I preserve & value above all she could else
have bequeathed me '.

Margaret's sweet relenting nature is shown in this
request to Godolphin ; a recompense, perhaps, for the
unhappiness Evelyn brought upon himself during the
last twelve months. But it is curious that Godolphin
made no mention of this request in a letter we shall
read presently ; moreover, she could hardly have
expected to bring the erstwhile rivals together in friendship. Yet it so happened — but not through her request.

Godolphin, still overcome with grief, was unable to
travel to Cornwall with the *cortège*. Evelyn, though
responsible for the funeral arrangements, rather surprisingly went only as far as Hounslow, being ' oblig'd
to return upon some indispensable affaires '.[1] These
affairs may well have been dealt with the following day,
when he and Godolphin (the latter concealing his
surprise that the other had avoided the final obsequies)
looked over and sorted Margaret's papers, letters and
meditations, and Evelyn was quick to recognize and
anxious to retrieve and conceal his own writings. But
he suffered disappointment ; none of them — for
which he had hurried back from Hounslow — came
to light. Among her effects, he says, was a ' small
packett seal'd-up, which she desir'd by the superscrip-
tion, might be burnt, and not open'd, as accordingly
it was performed, and as I conceive, might containe
the cipher, by which she us'd to correspond with

[1] *Diary*, 17th September 1678.

. . . the Dean of Hereford & some particulars which she would not trust her memory with, in case she had liv'd : for . . . she kept a register of mercys, deliverances, successes & resolutions . . . for the discussion of her conscience, with the most accurate niceness imaginable — but I enter no farther into this seacret '.[1]

Although Evelyn seems fairly well acquainted with this ' seacret ', may we not wonder whether the burnt packet contained Margaret's letters to Evelyn which she had asked him to return and which perhaps Godolphin, after all, had never read ? However that may be, the earlier meditations written by Evelyn for Margaret were found by Godolphin nine days later,[2] but whether or not they were read by him must remain his own secret.

The surviving series of letters written between Godolphin and Evelyn after Margaret's death seem more properly to belong to a study in patronage than of friendship ; nevertheless, the first in the series (22nd September 1678) may justifiably be quoted here, giving as it does, a hint that Evelyn, not Godolphin, was the originator of their friendship (and it therefore follows that Evelyn was more slighted in the Will than he would have us believe).

' Deare Mr Evelyn (for I hardly yett dare call you by that name which you had so much better bestowed) 'tis ye desire of my soule to become more worthy of itt, & ye greatest consolation my condition is capable off, to see you soe desirous of my friendship, & soe kind & good natur'd to promise me yours. A thousand things crowd into my mind to say to you, where shall I begin ? most naturally with my owne Interest ; I lay hold them

[1] *Life*, p. 83.   [2] Letter : Godolphin to Evelyn, 27th October 1678.

(to ye great joy & comfort of my spirit) of ye promise of your friendship & kindnesse ; I lay hold of it in ye manner you offer it to me, I desire to fill the place that she held with you, & O if it were ye will of ye Almighty that I might doe it worthyly. I promise you mine most faithfully & inviolably as long as I live, & I will keep your letter for ever as the pledge of your constant friendship to mee. I will remember you constantly in my prayers ; I must forgett to pray when I forgett you, or her, who (with your assistance & God Almighty's Grace, continually working with her) has taught me all that I know of Good, & made such impression of my duty as any soule, as I hope by ye grace of God I shall always preserve there, especially now Ye Almighty has putt it into your heart soe kindly to offer me your assistance for the cultivating of them ; 'tis that which I want, 'tis that which I would have wish'd of all earthly things, & if you will believe ye first profession of your friend, I look upon your letter as a beame of God Almighty's countenance, & an earnest of his future care & protection of me ; Remember then that from henceforth I look upon you as ye Depositary of all my concerns spirituall & temporall, to bee wholly guided & directed by you in ye former, to have always great regard to your opinion in ye latter. And now you see I have putt you just in ye place of her that I have lost, oh Losse ! never to bee enough by me lamented, never to bee supplyd on this side Heaven, my heart has been divided & almost rent between ye submission that I owe to God Almighty, & the ease that I seek (& for ye present perhaps should find) in giving the reins to my griefe : & at those times when I strive to suppress it, there comes one thought very often into mind which

I confesse to you troubles mee ; 'tis an apprehension I have least my sence of this losse (how great soever) will bee worne out by Time as wee see all impressions of this nature are in most people ; I have no patience to think it shall be soe ; I am almost at an end of my paper & of my time, but nott of my matter : I must contract ; ye worke which you meditate I doe not dislike, I commend it, I would not restraine you from the satisfaction & the entertainment of it : I would not bar my selfe the profitt & the delight of itt ; but by no means lett it goe farther I conjure you, at least for ye present, you & I will debate the matter when wee meet, in ye mean while I hope I shall heare of you sometimes, pray God blesse you & yours.'

The work which Godolphin mentions at the end of his letter is, of course, *The Life of Mrs. Godolphin.* Now, why should Evelyn write the history of Margaret's life, a life in which his own aspirations were so bitterly unfulfilled ? We have seen that she escaped him in life ; in death he would recapture her. In the new and promising interest of Godolphin's acceptance of his friendship, any sense of frustration or bitterness slowly faded, and in a resurgence of sublimation he now decided to translate her into a saint in print, from which there could be no second escape. In this act, in giving her glory which he would himself share, he would also put a halo on his disappointed head.

The writing of the *Life* was both arduous and tricky ; he had constantly to consider what others divined of its nuances. He spent more time than ever in his study ; on 22nd August 1682 Mrs. Evelyn told Bohun that ' he lives most part of the night in his hole '.

As his panegyric took shape, occasionally and

SIDNEY GODOLPHIN
From an engraving after the portrait by Sir Godfrey Kneller

characteristically he visited the baby Francis, rewarding
the nursemaid's submission to his importunity with
gifts of money at Easter and the New Year.[1]

Godolphin never married again. There were, however, rumours and indications of romantic attachments :
but there is no certainty that the sense of his loss of
Margaret, as he feared it might be, was eventually worn
out by time. Evelyn, playing his adulatory part, strove
hard to keep her virtues fresh in Godolphin's mind ;
every anniversary of her death was commemorated by
a letter to Godolphin in praise of ' their incomparable
saint '. It is true that Evelyn's tributes became more
brief as the years passed and the material benefits
mounted from his friendship with Godolphin. Accordingly, in the autumn of 1690, when the second of these
romantic attachments was reported, Evelyn found it
easy to approve :

'. . . For whilst I understand you have made choice
of a Lady so transcendently like her predecessor :
accomplish'd in all the vertues & ornaments she was
possess'd of, not onely my consent must be included in
it, but my highest approbation : There's one thing yet
to render your happy Lady, not onely the resemblance
but the very prototype, of that incomparable Saint,
but her very-selfe, remaining : That she accept of my
humble service & reguard me with some distinguishing
grace for the sincere honour & affection, I have ever
born to him, on whom she has placed hers so worthily —
which is all the merite I pleade ; And so God Almighty
give ye both joy.'[2]

[1] Account Book, 1679–81.
[2] Letter to Godolphin, 20th September 1690. For the rest of the imperfect evidence regarding Godolphin's attachments, see Appendix D in
Life : note the serious misprint, 1698 for 1678, on p. 237.

But doubtless Godolphin declared that Evelyn had been misinformed — as indeed he was — and that his honoured approbation was not yet called for.

When the *Life* was completed, Evelyn stayed his hand as advised by Godolphin, and kept it from the public eye. In 1685 or thereabouts he presented Lady Sylvius with a manuscript version (in response, he says, to her commands [1]), but Godolphin was barred its ' profit and delight ' until he became Lord Treasurer in May 1702, when Evelyn, with one foot in the grave, made him a congratulatory present of a slightly different manuscript version.

It is significant that no acknowledgment of either gift survives. Any acclamation would certainly have been preserved by Evelyn. There is little doubt that both Lady Sylvius and Godolphin penetrated the falsities of Evelyn's equivocal biography, as surely as we, with the aid of letters and meditations, have now done. Evelyn lived until 27th February 1706, having nearly four years in which to regret that his belated gift to Godolphin was not kept — as doubtless originally intended — as a bequest.

[1] *Life*, p. 8.

INDEX

THE END

PRINTED BY R. & R. CLARK, LTD., EDINBURGH